# A
# PICTORIAL BIOGRAPHY
of the
Venerable Master

# HSÜ YÜN

## Volume Two

# A
# PICTORIAL BIOGRAPHY
## of the
## Venerable Master

# HSÜ YÜN

## Volume Two

*Composed by*
*Venerable Master Hua*

Translated into English by

Buddhist Text Translation Society
Dharma Realm Buddhist University
Dharma Realm Buddhist Association

2003

*A Pictorial Biography of the Venerable Master Hsü Yün - Volume II*

**Published and Translated by:**

**The Buddhist Text Translation Society**
1777 Murchison Drive, Burlingame, CA 94010-4504

©2003   **Buddhist Text Translation Society**
        **Dharma Realm Buddhist University**
        **Dharma Realm Buddhist Association**

First Edition (USA) 1985
Second Edition (Malaysia) 2003

11 10 09 08 07 06 05 04 03      10 9 8 7 6 5 4 3 2 1

ISBN 0-88139-486-6

Printed in Malaysia

Addresses of the Dharma Realm Buddhist Association branches are listed
at the back of this book.


Library of Congress Cataloging-in-Publication Data

Hsuan Hua, 1908-
    Pictorial biography of Venerable Master Hsü Yün / composed by Venerable
Master Hsuan Hua.
        p. cm.
    ISBN 0-88139-485-8 (v.1) -- ISBN 0-88139-486-6 (v.2)
1. Xuyun, d. 1959. 2. Priests, Buddhist-China--Biography. I. Title.

BQ997.U98 H75 2003
    294.3'92'092--dc21
        [B]
                                                           2002074740

Namo Original Teacher Shakyamuni Buddha

# Contents

*In the past he fostered the roots of virtue,*
  *and so his Way-mind was resolute.*
*Leaving home as a pure youth,*
  *he traveled everywhere seeking good teachers.*
*With bones made of steel and stone,*
  *he forged ahead with vigorous momentum.*
*With vajra will and resolve,*
  *he boarded the prajna boat of patience.*

*He taught and transformed living beings*
  *using profound prajna wisdom.*
*He propagated the Buddhadharma,*
  *and entered Great Nirvana.*
*Everyone in the cosmos gazes up at him,*
  *in earnest admiration.*
*His renown lives on through the ages,*
  *illumining heaven and earth.*

verse by the Venerable Abbot Hua

This silly, decrepit old fool
Has lived a wretched, upside-down life.
Searching far and wide for a true friend,
Still he hasn't found one who knows his sound.
Shovelling snow, digging wells without ever resting;
Using a turtle's hair as pillars to build Way Places.
He's wasted the donor's funds and grains
And toiled for an entire life in vain.

"Roaming-in-Illusion Bhikshu," Hsü Yün.

This crazed fellow – where does he come from?
For no reason he sticks out his neck during
    the Dharma-ending Age.
Lamenting that the Sagely Path
    hangs by a precarious thread,
He cares not for his own affairs –
    for whom does he worry?
On a lonely mountain peak
He sends down a baited hook to catch a carp.
Plummeting to the depths of the ocean bed,
He stokes a fire to fry a sea bubble.
Not finding one who knows his sound,
He sighs in sorrow.
Yet his laughter pierces the void!
Scold him, he doesn't gripe.
Ask him: why don't you put it down?
"When will the masses' sufferings
    come to an end –
That's when I will rest!"

"Roaming-in-Illusion Bhikshu,"
composed at age 119
Yun Chü (Cloud Abode) Mountain

# Song Of The Skin Bag

By the Venerable Master Hsü Yün ("Empty Cloud," 1840-1959), who wrote this song at the age of nineteen and left it to his two wives when he escaped from his household to become a monk. The marriage to the two women was pressed upon him and never consumated in either case. Later, inspired and deeply moved by the Master's virtue in the Way, his two wives left home and became Bhikshunis.

Song of the Skin Bag,
    the skin-bag lament!
Before the Empty eon,
    it had no name or shape.
Since Buddha Awesome Sound,
    a hindrance it has been.
Three hundred sixty joints
    connect the body's frame.
Its every inch is covered by
    eighty-four thousand pores.
One of the triad of primal forces[1]
    combining the four great elements[2],
It holds up heaven and pillars earth
    – a spirit magnificent!
Because of cause and effect,
    discern the times.
Despite our view of past and present,
    muddled we remain –
All because of confused attachment
    to this illusory shape.
We tire out our parents, and

---

[1]  Heaven, earth, and people.
[2]  Earth, water, fire, and wind.

Cling to our wives and children.
Our vain ignorance leaves behind
    a trail of karmic debts.
Song of the Skin Bag,
    the skin-bag lament.
Drinking wine and eating meat
    confound the mental nature.
Indulging desires in greed for pleasure
    brings ruin in the end.
The higher the office, the greater
    influence and power to oppress;
Buying and selling is cheating people
    by means of craftiness.
Honor, wealth, extravagance
    – how long can they last?
When misfortune and poverty come,
    all is spent in an instant.
False discernment of self and others
    creates inequality.
By harming living things, we treat
    them as so many weeds.
And every day our reckoning's based on
    stupidity, anger, and greed.
Sinking in these perversities, we're
    destroyed entirely.
Recklessly we kill, steal, lust,
    lie.  Contemptuous
Of kin and friends, we're ravaged by
    love and hate.
Scolding the wind, cursing the rain,
    deriding the spirits and gods,
Not understanding birth and death,
    we're truly at a loss.
From a cow's belly born,
We enter the womb of a mare.
As heads and faces change,
    who praises his luck?

Who mourns his doom?
We create much evil,
But plant no blessings.
How vain our passage
    through birth and death!
How useless the clamor of our lives!
Thence, to the three evil paths:
We fall to the hells
Or suffer as ghosts or animals.
The sages of old
Kept wagging their tongues
Like morning chimes and evening drums,
Attempting to stir the
    strings of our hearts.
Retributions for good and evil are
    sharp and clear as can be.
They awaken us so that we want to
    leave the five-fold turbidity.
Song of the Skin Bag,
The skin-bag lament!
Endowed with form, let it not
    encumber you.
Illusory substance, mere false name,
    it's just a relative dharma.
Quickly turn your heart around,
    and contemplate at ease.
To kin bid farewell and sever all
    ties of love,
Withdraw from the world and leave.
Don't cling to wife,
Don't pine for children.
Enter the door of emptiness;[3]
    receive the Buddha's precepts.
Seek a bright teacher,
Ask for instruction.

---

3.   Buddhist monastery

Investigate Ch'an, meditate well,
Stop the climbing mind's insanity.
Once and for all, to the red dust
    wave goodbye.
Subdue the six senses,
Cut off thoughts.
Without self or others, afflictions cease.
Be not like the worldly,
    who sigh at the passing of mist and dew.[4]
A robe to shield you, food to fill you
    – enough to sustain your body's needs.
Riches and jewels renounce.
Look lightly on body and life.
Reject them as spit and phlegm,
    and do not hesitate!
Hold precepts purely,
Blemishless.
In four comportments be clear as ice
    and pure as jade.
When scolded,
Don't be angry;
    when beaten, do not hate.
Bear what is hard to bear.
Forget about mockery.  Overlook sarcasm.
Ignore both winter and summer.
Work without interruption.
From beginning to end, recite with
    a single mind "Namo Amita Buddha."
Do not lapse into torpor;
Refrain from getting scattered.
Be like the pine and the cypress,
    never fading, evergreen.
Doubt not the Buddha,
Doubt not the Dharma,
Wholesome knowledge is to

---

4.   The signs of impermanence, since mist and dew evaporate very quickly

understand what it is you hear and see.
Bore through the paper,
Pierce the cowhide.[5]
Do not err.  Make your mind
    round and bright.
Return to the origin;
Reach liberation.
Go back to the source,
    retrieve your heaven-true nature.
Nothing's not nothing;
Emptiness isn't empty:
The divine potential's revealed;
    its wonder hard to imagine.
You've arrived;
You haven't toiled in vain.
Just in that instant,
    for you it is finished.
You are rightfully given the name
"Great Hero."
You embody ten titles – perfect and bright
    – teaching ten thousand generations.
Ah!  The same leaking shell can now manifest
    bodies throughout ten directions!
With good and evil distinguished clearly,
    no more mistakes occur.
But why do you rely on
The false alone
And yet not practice the true?
The T'ai Chi  "absolute" divides
    into heaven and earth.
With a lively thrust, you should turn
The ch'ien and k'un[6] of your own mind.
Kings and prime ministers

---

5.   Bore through the pages of the Sutras and deeply penetrate to their meaning; cut through the thick covering of ignorance which is like cowhide.

6.   The Two Modes of the T'ai Chi: heaven and earth, light and dark, etc.

certainly practiced
The Way in previous lives.
Wealth and honor or utter poverty
    are due to people's past causes.
Once there is birth,
    death then will follow;
Everyone knows this. Why moan and gripe?
For wives and riches,
For heir and fortune,
You ruin your future.
    It's all due to anger and greed.
For what sort of profit, for what kind
    of fame have I wasted nineteen springs?[7]
A thousand matters are not as you
    wish them to be.
Embroiled in the world, you're assailed
    by hardships constantly.
Once old, your eyes grow dim,
    your hair turns snowy white.
With no particular virtue at all,
    you've wasted your whole life!
Days stretch to months,
Months reach to years.
In vain you lament the passage of time,
    rolling on and on like a wheel.
Who is immortal in this world?
Better return and bow to the One
    whose compassion is like a cloud.[8]
Visit the sacred mountains,
Places sublime,
Just as you wish, in comfort and ease.
Swiftly comes impermanence.
But do you know? Are you aware?

---

7. The Venerable Hsü Yün left the home-life at age nineteen.
8. The Buddha, who with his Dharma Cloud compassionately shields all living beings.

Just how much idle, empty chatter
    do you want to hear?
Recite "Amitabha!"
End birth and death.
Keep yourself happy.
How many can be like that?
Investigate dhyana,
Attain the purport of the School.[9]
In such endeavors there's boundless
    vigor and energy.
Plain tea, vegetarian food:
Let not your mind be greedy.
Throughout the day and night, rejoice.
Be happy in the Dharma.
Get rid of self and others,
    do away with this and that.
See that foe and friend are equal;
    forget about slander and praise.
Gone are impediments,
There's no shame or insult.
Achieve a mind like the Buddhas' and Patriarchs'.
What are you waiting for?
The Bhagavan cut the strings of love
    and climbed the snowy mountains.
Kuan Yin bade farewell to kin
    and became the Buddha's disciple.
At the time of Emperors Yao and Shun[10],
Hermits Ch'ao and Hsü passed their days.
When Yao offered Ch'ao the empire's rule,
Ch'ao washed his ears in the stream.[11]
Chang Tzu Fang and Liu Ch'eng Yi
Also gave up officialdom to roam
    the rivers and mountains.
Much more should we,

---

9.   School refers to the Ch'an School.
10.  Yao and Shun were two sagely kings of the Gold Age of China

In the Dharma's demise,
Fraught with anguish and difficulties,
Now strive to be like those of old
    in search of our enlightenment.
Indulging ignorance, creating ten evils,
We waste our resources,
    reap the world's scorn.
Weapons, armies, plagues, and droughts
    – much misery to be borne!
Famines and wars are more and more
    frequent at every turn.
The daily news is fearful,
    full of strange forebodings.
Earthquakes, tidal waves,
    devastating landslides:
What can we do while caught
    in this age and time?
This surely is the result of
    evil done in former lives.
Faced with such adversity,
    we can fall into worse confusion.
But poor and unfortunate,
    if we create a thought of goodness,
Such wholesome thoughts can help us
    enter a temple and bow to the Dharma King.
Repent and reform your offenses;
Then your blessings can grow.
Bow to a bright-eyed teacher,
    seek for certification.
End birth and death: see the mind,
    understand the nature.

---

11. Emperor Yao heard of the virtue of the two sages Ch'ao and Hsü and
wanted to abdicate in their favor, but both of them refused. In fact, when
Ch'ao Fu heard the offer, he was so displeased that he went to the stream to
wash out his ears. Hsü Yü, who was downstream tending his ox, had to move
upstream because he didn't want his ox to drink the water, which he said had
been polluted by the filth Ch'ao Fu washed out.

Smashing through impermanence is
    what we mean by permanence.
The path within the path is found
    through strong cultivation.
The sages and worthies bequeathed wise
    sayings and lucid exhortations.
Uphold the Tripitaka teachings
    with reverence.
Cleanse your heart; purge your
    inner workings.
Encourage people to guard what is proper.
Don't think my words are idle.
Don't fail to pay attention.
Great cultivators must see
    their own natures.
Quickly cultivate and be
    heroically vigorous.
Plant the proper causes of Bodhi;
Aim to be born in the nine lotus grades,
    to be certified by the Buddhas.
Let Amitabha Buddha
    take you to the West.
Put down the skin bag; ascend the
    utmost vehicle. That's the quest supreme.
The Song of the Skin Bag's sung.
    I urge you all to listen!

A picture taken at Monastery of the White-Robed One at Ning-p'o to commemorate the visit of the Venerable Hsü Yün, Dhyana Master Hung I, and others.

From left to right: Upasaka Chi Tz'u Huang; Great Master Huei Hsing; Venerable Ch'u Ch'en; Vinaya Master Hung I; Venerable Hsü Yün; Venerable Wen Chih; Great Master Hsiu Yuan; and, the Ascetic An Hsin.

# A Recollection of My Affinities with the Venerable Yun

## Shi To Lun

I am a monk from the Changbai (Eternally White) Mountains, a Chan cultivator from the Black Waters. I brought forth a resolve for the Way in my youth. Hearing of the filial piety of Filial Son Wang (Great Master Chang Ren) of Shuangcheng (Twin Cities) County, I vowed to emulate him. Every morning and evening, after bowing to the Buddhas, I bowed three times to my father and mother. At first, they thought it strange, but after a while they became used to it. Later on, I took refuge with the Triple Jewel and had deep faith in Buddhism. I went to study under Great Master Chang Ren (Filial Son Wang of Shuangcheng County). The Great Master's instructions to me were always right on the mark. After my mother died, I built a simple hut by her grave and had my head shaved, leaving the home-life.

Hearing that the Elder Venerable Hsu Noble Yun, a great wise advisor of the Chan school, was teaching in Nanhua Monastery at Caoxi, I wished to go there. However, that would have involved a difficult trek through mountainous terrain. After the Japanese surrendered in 1945, transportation became more convenient. In the fall of 1946, in the middle of the eighth lunar month, I packed my bags and set out with two disciples, Guo Neng and Guo Shun. (I have no news of Guo Neng. Guo Shun cremated himself as an offering to the Buddhas.) We headed for Caoxi, wishing to draw near the Venerable Master Yun. The journey was very arduous. We walked during the day and rested at night, sometimes travelling even at night, until we reached Prajna Monastery in Changchun (which was called Xinjing, "New Capital," during the Manchu Empire regime). My two disciples remained at that monastery, waiting to receive full ordination the following year. Without carrying any extra clothes or luggage (the clothes I wore didn't exceed five pounds), I travelled alone towards the interior.

When I reached Tianjin, I stayed at Great Compassion Temple and heard Elder Dharma Master Tanxu lecture on the Shurangama Sutra. I met Dharma Master Tijing and rode in the same boat with him to Proper Enlightenment Monastery in Hubei. Also travelling with us were Dharma Masters Shengzhao, Shengmiao, Zhaoding, Yuanxiang, Renhui, Benzhi, Jiaozhi, Yongling, Lingguan, Jingjie, and others.

I composed a verse which goes,

> Fourteen monks rode in the same boat.
> Honored and noble were they; only I was poor.
> Clad in ragged robes,
> I ate one meal and had no extra possessions.
> People could scold and slander me as they pleased.

At that monastery, I performed austerities and chores such as cleaning, boiling water, tending the garden, watching the door, taking care of the Buddha-hall, and serving as verger. My skill in Chan samadhi increased greatly. In 1947, after going to Mount Potola to receive full ordination, I went to study the doctrines at the Buddhist Academy at Lingyanshan Monastery in Suzhou. In the fall, I went to Kongqing Mountain to take part in a Chan session and pass the winter. I paid respects to Venerable Mingguan and Venerable Liaocheng. In the first month of 1948, I left for Shanghai and then took a boat to Baotong (Precious Penetration) Monastery in Hubei. When I boarded the boat, I was penniless. On the boat I met a cripple who couldn't walk. When I recited the Great Compassion Mantra to aid him, he was immediately healed and could walk again. This evoked respect and faith from the rest of the boat's passengers. Before parting, they donated over 700,000 fa bi (monetary units). Thus I was able to buy a train ticket to go to Qujiang. At the train station I met Master Jouyi, a native of Hubei. When I asked him, he told me he was also going to Nanhua Monastery in Guangdong to draw near the Venerable Master

Yun. I asked him, "Have you got money to buy a train ticket?" He said, "No." I bought him a ticket, and the two of us took the train to Maba. When we got off the train, Master Jouyi said, "I'm hungry." After paying for the train fare, I still had over 100,000 fa bi, which I gave to him to buy breakfast. Again, I was left penniless.

Upon reaching Nanhua Monastery, I bowed to Venerable Master Yun, feeling like an infant seeing his mother again, like a wandering son who returns home. After so many years of yearning admiration, I was finally able to fulfill my wish. When I first arrived, I was assigned to serve as verger in the Patriarch Hall. When Dharma Master Zhican came to visit, he and I found that we shared the same views on cultivation, and he recommended me to the Venerable Master Yun as a capable person and worthy vessel of Dharma. The Venerable Master Yun then summoned me to the Abbot's quarters and asked me to be Superintendent of the Vinaya Academy. I refused. He urged me three times. I said, "Your student has come ten thousand miles to meet the Good Knowing Advisor and in order to end birth and death. If the Venerable Master can guarantee that I will be able to end birth and death, then I wouldn't refuse your orders even if you told me to jump into a cauldron of boiling water, walk on fire, or give up my body and bones."

The Venerable Master Yun replied, "One ends one's own birth and death, just as one eats one's own food to fill oneself. If I were to say that I guaranteed that you will end birth and death, I'd be cheating you. I don't do that sort of thing. In cultivation, one should concentrate on inner skill and outer accomplishment. By cultivating both blessings and wisdom one will succeed. One should not be an independent Arhat, looking after only his own good. One should practice the Bodhisattva Way for the good of all, support the monastery, and be of service to everyone. In that way, one may perfect blessings and wisdom and quite naturally end birth and death." I again refused. The Venerable Master Yun said, "You came all the way from northeast China to meet me. If you are not going to obey my instructions, why did you bother to come at all?" I then accepted the position.

I carefully observed the words and actions of the Venerable Master Yun and found them to be quite ordinary. What set him apart from ordinary people was his ability to set an example for others with his own practice and his willingness to take suffering and hard work upon himself.

During the spring precept-transmission, when the morning boards were struck, I heard with my own ears the roar of a tiger at first nearby and then off in the distance. My Dharma friends told me, "That is the tiger who took refuge with the Venerable Master Yun and became his disciple. It lives in a cave behind the mountain and always comes out to protect the monastery during the precept ceremonies."

After the transmission of the precepts, the Venerable Master Yun returned quietly and alone to Yunmen, where he was supervising the construction of buildings. That summer, I went to the district of Nancheng in Jiangxi to lecture on the Amitabha Sutra at the invitation of Elder Layman Huang Juzai. I returned to Nanhua Monastery in the middle of the eighth month. In the middle of the ninth month, a group of bandits who were intent on ransacking the monastery broke down the door and entered the Nanhua Vinaya Academy. When I went out to meet them, they pointed their guns at my chest and said, "We're going to shoot you." I said, "Why do you want to shoot me?" The bandits said, "Because you didn't open the door." I said, "I didn't open the door because you have come to rob me, not to give me gifts. If you had been in my place, you wouldn't have dared to open the door either." The bandits said, "Hand over your money!" I pointed at my ragged robe and said, "Look! Would someone wearing such tattered clothes have money?" The bandits asked, "Well, who does?" I said, "I'm the Dharma Master here, and all the rest are student monks. If I am penniless, surely they will be poorer yet. This room is where I live. You are welcome to look around and take whatever you like." Hearing me conversing with the bandits as if nothing were going on, Dharma Master Huaiyi came out from the inner rooms to join the conversation. The bandits promptly let go of me and seized him, giving him the same treatment they had given me. Master Huai burst into tears and hung his head, afraid to look up. The thieves then said, "Give us your money!" Master Huai said, "Go to my room and get it." They entered his room and took everything in it, leaving it empty.

The following day at class, Master Huai announced to the students, "Of the hundred or more monks at Nanhua Monastery, only one man showed no sign of fear – Dharma Master To Lun." When it came time for me to teach, I said, "Master Huai said I was the only one in this monastery who was not afraid. He was wrong. As far as I know, there were four people: First of all, the Sixth Patriarch, Great Master Huineng, sat unmoving in bright samadhi, without worrying or paying any attention, as if nothing were going on. Second, Patriarch Hanshan sat erect, nourishing his spirit with eyes closed, in a state of internal and external emptiness in which concepts of self and others were both gone. Third, Patriarch Dantian stuck out his head to take a look around and see what was going on, yet did not say a single word. The fourth one was me, the mountain monk To Lun, who not only looked but also spoke. I conversed with the thieves and got all excited, but I was not afraid either." After I said this, the class broke into laughter.

The news soon reached the Venerable Master Yun, who hurried back from Yunmen and called a general meeting. Present at the meeting were Dharma Masters Huaiyi and To Lun, and the Venerable Master Yun himself chaired the meeting. There were over thirty students, including Zuyin, Yunmiao, Wuyun, Xuanyang, Hengding, Tihui, Tiguang, Faliang, Hailong, Fahui, Wanxin, Zhikong, Faming, and Fakai. After the incident of the bandits, everyone in the monastery was unsettled and wished to leave. The Venerable Master Yun urged Master Huai to stay on, but he refused. He tried to detain the students, but they wouldn't listen. Under these circumstances, he broke down and wept bitterly. He said, "To the end of time, I will never again run a Buddhist Academy." Then he got up and returned to the Abbot's quarters. I was deeply moved and vowed to assume the duties of managing and continuing to run the Buddhist Academy. Later Master Huai went to Guangxi, and I became solely responsible for all the classes at the Nanhua Vinaya Academy.

On New Year's Day of the following year (1949), I wrote a letter to the Venerable Master Yun resigning from my post as Dean of Academic Affairs at the Academy. I then stayed in the Tripitaka Hall and read the Tripitaka (Buddhist Canon). During the precept-trans-mission I was asked to be one of the certifying acharyas. Afterwards, I went with Venerable Master Yun to Dajian Monastery in Shaoguan. When Venerable Master Yun then suggested that I continue with him to Yunmen, I agreed to join him there but insisted on first returning to Nanhua. In the beginning of the fifth month, I set out for Dajiao Monastery (in Yunmen). The mountainous path was winding and narrow, similar to the roads in Sichuan province. Night fell when I was about twenty li from Yunmen. Since I was travelling alone, it was difficult to make progress on the unfamiliar path. Suddenly a lamp-light appeared before me, and I followed it. The light remained at a constant distance of about a hundred paces before me, and when I finally reached it, it disappeared. Looking around, I discovered that I had arrived at the very gate of Dajiao Monastery. Everyone had already retired. I knocked on the door, entered, and saw the Venerable Yun, who asked, "Why did you arrive so late?" I told him the reason and described how I had been guided by a lamp-light. The Venerable Yun said, "How remarkable! It is difficult enough to travel on these mountain roads during the day without a guide. How remarkable that you have been able to find your way in the pitch black of night! Very strange!" After arranging a place for me to stay, the Venerable Yun said, "You were the panshou (head of the assembly) at Nanhua, and you should continue to be the panshou at Yunmen. You should lead the assembly to cultivate during ceremonies, at mealtime, and sitting in meditation."

I had not been at Yunmen very long when I became ill because of the dampness of the weather. It was very hard to bear, and so I requested leave from the Elder Master to return to Guangzhou to recuperate. The Venerable Yun refused and said, "Don't go. If you do, it will be difficult to return." I said, "No. Your disciple has already made up his mind. He is definitely going." Hearing my words, the Elder Master was grieved to the point of tears. He took my hand and said, "If you go, we will not be able to meet again." I said, "I'll return as soon as my illness is healed. Please don't worry about me!" The Elder Master said, "After you have left, you should make every effort on behalf of Shakyamuni Buddha and establish Way-places to carry on the work of the Patriarchs of the past. The future is very bright. Push on, work hard. Conduct yourself well, and don't disappoint me. Take care. Goodbye."

I travelled to Guangzhou and then to Hong Kong, where I stayed at East Potola Monastery. In the seventh month, I returned to Guangzhou and stayed at Liurong Monastery. The Abbot Mingguan asked me to serve as the hall manager and assistant manager of the monastery. Since I planned to return to Yunmen after the mid-autumn festival (the fifteenth of the eighth month) I agreed to serve for the time being. But in the beginning of the eighth month, Shaoguan fell and the road was cut off, making it impossible to go back. On the night of the eighteenth of the eighth month, Xie Kuanhui and Chen Kuanman paid for my boat fare and I went to Hong Kong again. I travelled to Thailand to examine the southern transmission of Buddhism. In 1950 I returned to Hong Kong and went into seclusion in Guanyin Cave. I was as if deaf and dumb. Each time I thought of the Elder Master Yun's parting words, I regretted not having listened to the Good Knowing Advisor's advice. I wanted to go back to see the Elder Master, but it was impossible. Alas! What could be said? In the winter of 1951, I worked on the construction of Western Bliss Gardens (Xileyuan) Monastery. At the request of Luo Guoming, Chen Guofa, Tang Guoshan, Mai Guolian, Yuan Guolin, and other laypeople, I lectured on the Earth Store Sutra at Tongshan Temple. In the fall of the following year, I lectured on the Vajra Sutra at that Temple. The fall after that, I lectured on the Amitabha Sutra at Baojue (Precious Enlightenment) Monastery. Later on I delivered a fourteen-month lecture series on the Shurangama Sutra at Western Bliss Gardens Monastery. Later I lectured on the Earth Store Sutra at another temple. I worked on the construction of Cixing Chan Monastery and had an image of the Venerable Master Yun carved as a token of my utmost reverence. I wrote to the Venerable Yun and received from him a document entitled "The Treasury of the Orthodox Dharma Eye: The Source of the Buddhas and Patriarchs" – the Dharma of the mind-to-mind seal which is transmitted outside the teaching, the wonderful mind of Nirvana, the real mark which is without marks, the true emptiness which is not empty. Following the intent of the Patriarchs above and teaching living beings below, I was constantly mindful of the deep kindness of this Dharma-milk. The Elder Master wrote to me, urging me to do meritorious works. I vowed to contribute several tens of thousands of dollars to pay for the Buddha images in the Jewelled Hall of Great Heroes of Zhenru Chan Monastery at Yunju Mountain. I also travelled to Burma and purchased more than three hundred large cartons of gold foil for gilding the Buddha images. The Venerable Yun was very happy and wrote repeatedly in thanks. This shows the vast extent of the Venerable One's deep concern for the younger generation. He is humble and never careless. He denies himself everything to be generous to others and renounces his own will to comply with that of others. His awe-inspiring spirit, his matchless compassion, his lofty virtue, and his absolutely genuine impartiality cause people to serve him happily and willingly.

I received another letter from the Venerable Yun instructing me to return to Yunju Mountain. While in Chan contemplation I came to know that the Elder Master wished to transfer the responsibilities of Zhenru Monastery to me, but for various reasons I could not heed the command. Even now my regret knows no bounds. The Buddhist Lecture Hall had just been established, and every day I was busy with the work of propagating the great Dharma. Since there was no way I could be in two places at the same time, I planned to go back to be with the Elder Master and attend upon him after I had taken care of matters satisfactorily and found someone to assume my responsibilities in Hong Kong.

In July of 1959, I received news of the Venerable Yun's grave illness, and day and night I was worried. I knew it was an inauspicious sign. I had noticed in the Venerable One's Dharma portrait of 1958 that his eyes gazed out upon us and his eyebrows were several inches long, so they could have been tucked behind his ears. When I saw the portrait I bowed before it and was moved to say, "Every time the Venerable One closes his eyes for photographs, but this time the compassionate eyes are gazing on living beings. This is very unusual. It must be an indication of a major change. In less than a year it will be clear." Then I requested the greatly virtuous Sangha of the ten directions to bow, on behalf of the Elder Master Yun, the Jewelled Repentance of Medicine Master Buddha Who Dispels Calamities and Lengthens Life. I also arranged for several days of Universal Bowing to the Buddhas, and put a notice in the newspaper to let all the Elder One's disciples know, so that by the combined strength of the assembly's determination and sincerity a response would come to pass. At the time, I said to the assembly, "I fear that this is the last opportunity for us to practice Universal Bowing before the Buddhas, to bow the Medicine Master Repentance, and to perform other ceremonies for the Elder Master Yun." My voice was so laden with sorrow as I spoke these words that those who heard me also wept silently.

Then a letter came from Yunju saying: "The Venerable One is a little better. We are deeply relieved!" I immediately concentrated all my attention on finding an artist who could be commissioned for the painting of the Elder One's Pictorial Biography. The biography includes over two hundred exquisite Chinese brush drawings. In several tens of thousands of words, it sets forth the Elder One's life of superior virtue, his conduct and vows, the hardships he suffered, his toil, and his singular energy and spirit. The Elder Master is shown as an eternal model and guide for the sages to come. There has not been a model such as he in thousands of years. Unfortunately, death is inevitable. On October 16 (the fifteenth of the ninth lunar month), I received a telegram saying that on October 12 at 1:45 p.m., the Venerable One had completed the stillness at Zhenru Chan Monastery on Yunju Mountain. His instructions for those who would come after him were to diligently cultivate precepts, samadhi, and wisdom, and put to rest greed, anger, and stupidity; to forget themselves for the sake of the Dharma; to respect one another; and so forth.

When I heard this news, suddenly not only did the mountains collapse and the earth quake, but the whole world and everyone in it disappeared as the disaster of fire blazed through everything. I could not tell if I was dreaming or awake, if things were real or illusory. I was as dull as a puppet, as senseless as a clay image. After a while, when I came to my senses, I experienced an overwhelming grief. The next day, on the morning of October 17, I called together all the temple's donors to discuss arrangements for the memorial services. We decided to hold a 21-day Buddha Recitation Session followed by a 120-day Great Prajna Recitation Session. We hoped in this way to commemorate the Elder Master and to repay him for the kindness of the Dharma-milk he had given us. Then we sent telegrams overseas to inform Dharma companions in various parts of the world. Among those contacted were the Buddhist Lecture Hall in San Francisco; the Buddhist Association of Honolulu; Layman Li Juncheng and Laywoman Bi Junhui and others in Hawaii; Layman Zhan Liwu in Canada, and other disciples in Taiwan, Burma, Thailand, India, Ceylon, and other countries; and Layman Yu Jendong, Chairman of the World Buddhist Friendship Association. More than one hundred telegrams were sent out, and thus disciples throughout the world gathered in response to commemorate the Nirvana of the Elder One. Hong Kong Buddhists were contacted by phone, and on October 18, the newspapers in Hong Kong published the news.

Who would have thought that this would arouse people's jealousy! Evildoers began to slander and demonic ghosts went mad. They became so totally confused that they did not distinguish clearly what they saw and heard. Those self-proclaimed "Good Advisors" cleverly convinced not only themselves but impartial bystanders to follow along and join in their campaign. How pitiful! It is easy to believe the saying, "When deeds are good, the demons abound."

When all is said and done, I leave it for the Venerable Yun to decide: Have I done right? When Confucius wrote the Spring and Autumn Annals, the corrupt officials and thieves recoiled in dread. When Sima wrote the Historical Records, his exposes put an end to villains and criminals. I will devote all my strength to the Venerable Yun. Although ten thousand spears may pierce my body, I am absolutely not afraid. Proceed to aim your machinations at me. I will gladly withstand them. Great Master Yongjia said,

> "Contemplate vicious words,
> as merit and virtue.
> Then vicious words
> become one's Good and Wise Advisors.
> Do not let abuse and slander
> arouse enmity or liking.
> How else can the power of compassion and patience
> with non-production be manifest?"

He also said,

> "Let others slander me;
> I bear their condemnation.
> Those who try to burn the sky
> only exhaust themselves.
> When I hear it,
> it's just like drinking sweet dew.
> Thus smelted and refined,
> suddenly one enters the inconceivable."

Therefore, everyone should be aware of the inconceivable functioning of the law of cause and effect and of the inconceivability of the resulting retribution. Take heed! When you fall into the Hell of Pulling Tongues, it will be too late to regret what you have done.

On the fourth day of the tenth lunar month, I sent two lay disciples, Xie Guofeng and Ma Guoxian, to Yunju to receive a portion of the Elder Master Yun's sharira (relics) and bones and bring them back so we could make offerings to them. On the seventh, the two disciples arrived at Zhenru Chan Monastery and obtained more than ten sharira of rare brilliance, which emitted a light of five colors. They set out on the return trip on the sixteenth and arrived at the Lecture Hall on the afternoon of the eighteenth. I led the great assembly in offering incense and flowers and making prostrations to the sharira. Everyone was extremely happy, and I felt as if a great burden had been lifted off my shoulders.

The next day four laymen – Mao Wenda, Li Jungyou, Xie Guofeng, and Ma Guoxian – accompanied me to take the sharira and call on the Elder Layman Chen to discuss the publication of a memorial book. Layman Chen suggested that the publication be delayed to allow time for the receipt of articles from overseas. Thus it is only now that this book has been published and circulated. I hope that Buddhists in all countries of the world will unite in spirit and respect one another.

The Elder Yun's verse of bequest reads:

"Out of kind regard for the life of ants,
　　the shrimp don't hop back in the water.
That I might pacify aquatic creatures,
please toss my body in the river.
I pray that all who partake of my offering of body and
　　vows, will in turn attain Bodhi and rescue living beings.
I hope that my Dharma companions will not be sad
　　or worried about me.
Birth and death follow our karma,
　　just as the cocoon binds the silkworm that has spun it.
If you do not put an end to greed and confusion,
　　you will remain entrapped by joy and sorrow.
If you wish to be rid of this trouble,
　　you should cultivate diligently and refine yourself
Until a wonderful tallying with the unproduced occurs and
　　you gain a thorough understanding of the mind ground.
Through cutting off the emotions of love and hate,

you can be released from the dangerous turning wheel.
As you work to purify the three studies,
    firmly hold to the four dwellings in mindfulness.
When your vows are perfected, your body is
    as illusory as a dew drop or a lightning flash.
When you certify and awaken to true emptiness,
    the myriad dharmas become one substance.
Separation and union, sadness and joy,
    are as unsubstantial as bubbles.
After I die and my body is cremated,
Please take the ashes of my bones
And grind them into a fine powder.
Mix the powder with oil, sugar, and flour,
Roll it into pellets and then place these in the river
As an offering to the aquatic creatures.
I will be forever thankful if you grant my wish.
Hsu Yun, one who repays his debts, bows in reverence."


Let us take this as our standard of conduct and continue advancing towards the Buddha-city, never retreating from our resolve to realize anuttarasamyaksambodhi.

# Verse In Praise Of The Old Master's Image

The Venerable Master Hsü Yün
("Empty Cloud") at 119 years.

The revival of the Buddha's law came from the noble Yün,
Who also glorified the schools and the Dharma-doors.
The Sangha all relied upon and drew near to him.
Thus, the Triple Jewel dwells in the world, reaching all beings.
'Tho I'm an unschooled mountain-dwelling Sangha member,
I've received in transmission the seal of the Wei-yang line.
"Thus it is, thus it is, and once more, it is thus."
We only pray that you will look with kind eyes
        upon all living beings.

Reverently composed by
Disciple-in-Dharma-Transmission, To Lun

The Venerable Hsü Yün, at 120 Years
Three months before he completed the stillness

"Taking what others cannot take,
doing what others cannot do,
he endured what others cannot endure."

*A*
# PICTORIAL BIOGRAPHY
*of the*
# *Venerable Master*
# HSÜ YÜN

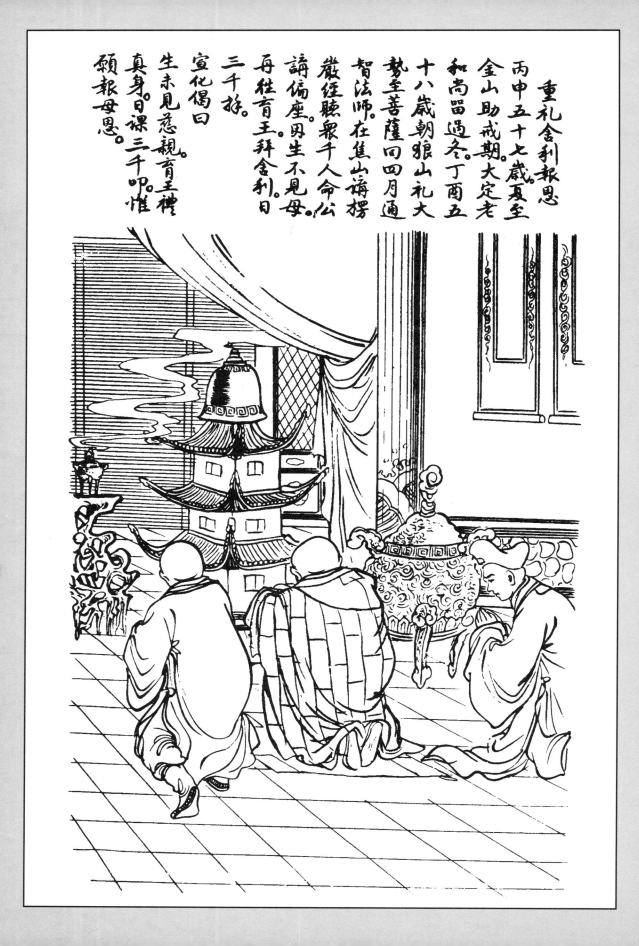

重礼舍利報恩

丙申五十七歲夏至
金山助戒期大定老
和尚留過冬丁酉五
十八歲朝狼山礼大
勢至菩薩回四月通
智法師在焦山諦聽
嚴經聽眾千人命公
講偏座男生不見母
母往育王拜舍利
二千拜
宣化偈曰
生未見慈親育王禮
真身日課三千叩。惟
願報母恩。

# 105

## Bowing again to the Sharira to repay his mother's kindness

During the summer of his fifty-seventh year, the Master went to Gold Mountain to assist with the transmission of the precepts. The Venerable Abbot Ta Ting (Great Concentration) requested that he stay for the winter as well. When the Master was fifty-eight years of age, he made a pilgrimage to Lang (Wolf) Mountain, in order to bow to Great Strength Bodhisattva. Upon his return, during the fourth lunar month, Dharma Master T'ung Chih (Penetrating Wisdom) requested that the Master aid him in explaining the *Shurangama Sutra* at Chiao (Parched) Mountain to an assembly of over one thousand people. Because the Master had never seen his mother, he decided to go again to Ashoka Monastery where he bowed to the sharira of the Buddha more than three thousand times a day.

It was said:

> From birth,
>     he never saw his mother,
> So at Ashoka Temple,
>     he bowed to the True Body.
> Every day,
>     he made three thousand prostrations,
> Only hoping
>     to repay his mother's kindness.

騎金龍見生母

忽一夜禪觀中。似夢
非夢見一金龍飛至。
長數丈金光晃耀公
騎之騰空至一山水
秀麗花木清出樓閣
宮殿莊嚴出見母
在樓閣上瞻眺公大
呼母親請你騎上龍
來到西方去龍降夢
醒。

宣化偈曰

飛龍在天見大人空
中樓閣幻即真請母
同往西方去夢醒依舊坐蓮臺

# 106

## Riding a golden dragon and seeing his mother

One night, while absorbed in dhyana meditation, in a dream which wasn't a dream, the Master suddenly saw a flying golden dragon alight. It was several tens of feet long and glittered with golden light. The Master mounted the dragon and ascended through the sky to a dark green wooded area, which flourished with flowers of rare beauty. There were exquisitely adorned palaces and pagodas everywhere. He saw his mother gazing out from one of the pagodas and called to her, "Come mount the dragon so we can fly to the West!" As the dragon descended, the Master suddenly returned to ordinary awareness.

The gatha says:

> A flying dragon came from the heavens
> and spied a noble man.
> Illusory pagodas and towers in empty space
> appeared to be real enough.
> He invited his mother to accompany him
> to the Western Land.
> When the vision was over, he was sitting as before
> – alone on a mat of straw.

扶疾燃指供佛

有許舍利皆參加眾
說非一公至十月末。
豆紫黑毛至十月末。
兩藏拜完再看大以
前變赤珠有光再急
弟看舍利大如黃豆
黃白各半始信因根
境示現十一月初大
病不能坐十六日有
八人約燃指公決參
加燃指病六愈
宣化偈曰 顯現宗旨大
慈仁助人燃指救道心風願
克遂真快樂本使已暢章雅容。

# 107

## Despite his sickness, burning off his finger as an offering to the Buddha

The Master joined some people who were bowing to the Buddha's sharira. Each of them saw it differently. When he first observed it, it was the size of a green bean and magenta in color. However, by the middle of the tenth month, after bowing in respect to the two Pitakas, he again viewed the relic. This time it had grown in size and appeared as a glowing red pearl. The Master was elated and began to bow. The sharira was now half yellow and half white and the size of a yellow bean. He was beginning to see how the same situation appears differently to each person according to his disposition. By the first day of the eleventh lunar month, the Master had become so ill he could not even sit up. He was one of a group of eight people, each of whom vowed to burn off a portion of a finger as an offering to the Buddha on the sixteenth day of the month. The Master was determined to take part, and recovered from his illness!

The gatha says:

> Bhikshu Hsien Ch'in (Apparent Relative)
>     and Bhikshu Tsung Liang (Bright Honor)
>     were men of great compassion.
> They aided those who burned their fingers
>     to mark their resolve on the Way.
> Enabled to fulfill his vow of the past,
>     the Master was truly joyous.
> His earnest wish thus completed,
>     he became quite peaceful and calm.

登雲台而望東海

乙亥六十歲應結森
寶林邀赴丹陽偏仙
台觀至句客赤山法
忍付茅蓬庚子六十
一歲扣舟朝五台入
終南修隱先到揚州
朝雲台山此山位於
江蘇山東昆崙高
入雲際放名雲台

宣化偈曰

東海名山古雲台。無
邊波浪入眼來煩惱
狼生何時度菩提佛
果力培栽。

# 108

## Climbing Yün T'ai[1] and viewing the sea

In his sixtieth year, the Master responded to the invitation of Dharma Masters Chieh Shen (Luxuriant Accumulation) and Pao Lin (Jeweled Forest) to come to Tan Yang (Red Sun) and help renovate Hsien T'ai Kuan (Immortals' Tower and Terrace) Temple. From there, he went to Chu Jung, where he used the hut of Dharma Master Fa Jen (Dharma Patience) of Ch'ih (Red) Mountain. When sixty-one years of age, the Master decided to make another pilgrimage to Wu T'ai (Five Peaks) Mountain, and then sequester himself on Chung Nan Mountain. He first went to Yang Chou to visit Yün T'ai (Cloud Terrace) Mountain, which lies on the border of Chiang Su and Shan Tung Provinces. Its height scales the clouds, which is why it was named Cloud Terrace.

The gatha says:

> The famous mountain on the Eastern Sea,
>     is the ancient Cloud Terrace,
> Where boundless waves on the ocean
>     are always in view.
> When will the myriad afflicted beings
>     all be crossed over?
> They must steadily nourish Bodhi
>     to attain the fruit of Buddhahood.

---

[1.] "Cloud Terrace"

登泰山觀天下
山東泰安縣城北。高
四十里之東嶽泰山。
乃五嶽名山之一。以
為歷代聖帝明君登
山山祭祀上帝玉皇。
因陀羅王之地山上
古蹟名勝不可勝數
有觀世音菩薩隆容
呼娘拋繡投繡諱搭
宣化偈曰
雲台朝罷登泰山天
下蒼生顛倒顛惟請
觀音哀憫授繡諱搭
諦到彼岸。

# 109

## Climbing Mount T'ai and observing the world

North of the cities of T'ai An (Peaceful) County, Shan Tung (Eastern Mountain) Province, lies the forty-*li* high Eastern Range, or T'ai Mountain, one of the well known five sacred mountains of China. Through the ages, the emperors and enlightened rulers ascended this mountain and made their sacrifices to Lord God – the Jade Emperor, the God Indra – for this was where they offered up the sacrifices. The ancient ruins on the mountain and the famous beautiful spots are uncountably many. There is the Temple of Avalokiteshvara (Kuan Yin) Bodhisattva – who is commonly referred to as a goddess – where many people come to offer incense.

The gatha says:

> Having made a pilgrimage to Cloud Terrace Mountain,
>     he ascended Mount T'ai.
> Millions and millions of living beings
>     are pitifully upside-down.
> He sought the response of Avalokiteshvara
>     to compassionately gather them in.
> Gate, gate, paragate,
>     arrival at the other shore.

11

朝訪那羅延窟

大方廣佛華嚴經云。
震旦國有山名那羅
延窟山有無量菩薩。
止住說法即指此處。
位於山東半島盡頭
勞山明高僧憨山老
人在此窟側建海印
寺後被道士毀壞電
气痕迹尚存在矣。
宣化偈曰
大方廣佛華嚴經那
羅延窟早説明今量
菩薩正演法有像狼
生入化中。

# 110

## Visiting Narayana Cave

The *MahaVaipulya Buddha Avatamsaka (Great Means Expansive Buddha Flower Adornment) Sutra* says: "There is a mountain in China called Narayana Cave Mountain where limitless numbers of Bodhisattvas who expound the Dharma dwell." The place referred to in the Sutra is situated at the tip of the Shan Tung Peninsula, on Lao Mountain. Near the cave, the eminent Ming Dynasty Sanghan, the Venerable Master Han Shan (Silly Mountain), established Hai Yin (Sea Seal) Monastery, which was later completely ruined by the Taoists. Today, not so much as a trace of it remains.

The gatha says:

> In the MahaVaipulya Buddha Avatamsaka Sutra,
>   very clearly,
> The Narayana Cave was mentioned
>   quite some time ago.
> There, limitless numbers of Bodhisattvas
>   right now proclaim the Dharma,
> And living beings who have the affinities
>   enter into the Teachings.

曲阜縣曉孔廟

儒教大成至聖孔子
廟乃中國文化創始
者。孔丘之紀念廟宇
也。位於山東曲阜縣
對於中國歷史文化
具重要性之價值公
以仰慕孔仲尼道德
文章故來此觀禮孔
廟孔陵以示意。
宣化偈曰
大哉孔子道德高高
世千秋皆師表三千
門人沐教化七十學
者入門墙。

**111**

## Visiting the Temple of Confucius in Ch'ü Fu County

The achievements of Confucius are extremely sagely and great, and Confucianism is an important element of Chinese civilization. The hall commemorating Confucius is located in Ch'ü Fu County, Shan Tung Province, and it holds a very important place in the history of Chinese culture. The Master greatly admired Confucius' Way virtue and scholarship, so he went there to view and pay his respects to the temple and tomb of Confucius in order to demonstrate these feelings.

The gatha says:

> Great indeed is Confucius,
>     whose virtue in the Way is high.
> A myriad generations for thousands of years
>     look to him as a teacher and model.
> Of more than three thousand pupils
>     whom this Master taught,
> There were but seventy scholars
>     who entered the door of his school.

宿棺盡遇亢人不懼

西行途中。夜宿破廟
祇一棺盡仰。知会人。
宿盡上事夜棺中大
動数次有聲曰我要
出来向你是人是鬼。
曰是人问是甚麼人。
曰是討飯的公发起。
令出。狀醜如鬼小解
復瞳天曙公行。

宣化偈曰
性定魔伏朝々樂。
念不起處々安正大
光明無所畏待人如
己有何分。

## 112

## Spending the night on a coffin cover, meeting a beggar, but not being frightened

The Master walked westward, and, at nightfall, he came upon a dilapidated temple in which there was nothing but a coffin, its cover upside down. Assuming that no one was inside, the Master slept on top. At midnight, however, he felt something moving around inside the coffin. "Let me out!" said a voice. The Master asked, "Are you a man or a ghost?" "I'm a man," was the answer. "Who are you?" asked the Master. "I'm a beggar," was the reply. The Master chuckled and got up, letting out a man who was ugly as a ghost. The beggar went out to urinate, and then went back to sleep. At dawn, the Master left.

The gatha says:

When the nature is in samadhi,
    the demons are quelled, and every day is joyful.
When false thoughts do not arise,
    every place is peaceful.
Bright and imposing was the Master's light
    – there was not a thing to fear.
If one treats people as oneself,
    what distinction is there?

步康莊連鬼兵怖驚
斯時義和團作亂山
東各縣一日正行路
中遇一洋兵以槍相
向。向公怕死否公曰
倘于該死汝手任便。
洋鬼兵見公神毛不
動。不驚不怖曰好的
你去。公遂趕赴五台。
行香畢以亂故回平。
宣化偈曰
卒然臨之不恐驚祇
緣因果已分清殺人
償命毫不錯欠債還
錢律不容。

# 113

## Meeting a mercenary on the highway
## but not being intimidated

Chaos prevailed in the counties of Shan Tung Province at this time due to the Boxer Rebellion. One day, the Master encountered a foreign soldier while walking down the road. The soldier pointed his gun at him and asked the Master: "Are you afraid of dying?" The Master replied, "If I am fated to die by your hand, then proceed." When the foreign soldier saw that the Master was not flustered, and that he was not to be intimidated or scared, he said, "Okay, you may go." The Master then quickly proceeded on to Wu T'ai Mountain. After offering up incense, he returned to Peking, due to the disturbance in Shan Tung.

The gatha says:

> Suddenly accosted by the mercenary,
>     the Master was unafraid,
> Only because cause and effect
>     is already clearly decided.
> For killing someone, one repays with one's
>     own life – it's not off in the slightest.
> To have a long-time standing debt and yet
>     refuse to pay is impermissible.

西域寺石刻藏經

河北省房山縣距離北京西南一百餘里。乃著名古剎歷代有聖僧應化清初圓通和尚主化其寺山頂有石藏經洞刻全部藏經乃隋靜晚法師創始歷唐宋元始竣工禮拜者頗多。宣化偈曰

靜晚刻經石壁間庵宋元朝始全扁正法久住醒迷夢般若恆明覺癡泯。

# 114

## Paying homage to the stone-carved Tripitaka at Hsi Yu[2] Monastery

Over one hundred *li* southwest of Peking, in Fang Shan County, Ho Pei Province, there is a well-known ancient shrine, where past generations of sagely Sanghans made their appearances. During the first years of the Ch'ing Dynasty, the Venerable Master Yüan T'ung (Perfect Penetration) headed the monastery there. On the mountaintop, there is a cave in the rocks, in which the entire Tripitaka is carved into the stone. The work was initiated by Dharma Master Ching Wan of the Sui Dynasty, and continued through the T'ang, Sung, and Yüan Dynasties until it was finished. The number of people who have gone there to worship is great indeed.

The gatha says:

> Bhikshu Ching Wan carved the Sutras
>    on the walls of stone.
> During T'ang, Sung, and Yüan times,
>    the entire Canon was then completed.
> The Proper Dharma long dwells
>    to rouse confused dreamers.
> Prajna wisdom, constantly bright,
>    awakens people from delusion.

---

[2.] Western Country

戒台寺礼飛鉢祖塔
至潭拓山訪異行僧。
戒台寺礼飛鉢禪師
祖塔紅螺參加念佛
道場。相傳明僧結茅
隱跡山中敬建道場。
飛鉢入皇宮太后見
之以金滿鉢中鉢
即飛四浮金俯戒台
寺置沉香龍鉢十座。
宣化偈曰
飛鉢化緣入皇宮太
后布施金滿盈以此
高等戒台寺沉香龍
鉢十師宗。

# 115

## Paying his respects to the stupa of Patriarch Fei Po[3] at Chieh T'ai[4] Monastery

When he reached T'an Che Mountain, the Master called on Bhikshu Yi Hsing (Extraordinary Practice), and at Chieh T'ai (Precept Platform) Monastery, bowed to the stupa of Patriarch Dhyana Master Fei Po (Flying Bowl). At Hung Lo (Red Conch), he participated in a Buddha recitation session. Legend has it this eminent Sanghan lived in a thatched hut on that mountain. Wishing to establish a Way place, he sent a flying bowl into the royal palace. When the Empress saw it, she filled the bowl to the brim with gold. The bowl then flew back to that Dhyana Master, who used it to build Chieh T'ai (Precept Platform) Monastery. He constructed dragon-thrones made of sink-in-water incense (aloeswood)[5].

The gatha says:

> The begging rounds of the flying bowl
> > took it into the royal palace,
> Where the Empress made a donation
> > of one full bowl of gold.
> Precept Platform Temple
> > now stately stands
> With its sink-in-water incense dragon thrones,
> > one for each Master of the Ten Schools.

---

[3.] "Flying Bowl"
[4.] "Precept Platform"
[5.] A very rare and fragrant wood which sinks when placed in water, hence its name.

大鐘寺觀古蹟。
大鐘寺觀明朝姚廣
孝所鑄八萬四千斤
銅鐘高於教層樓宇。
紐高七尺徑一丈四
尺外鑄華嚴經全部
內法華經全部尊勝
咒全部以金剛經鎖
邊其紐楞嚴咒為永
樂帝存母而造也。
宣化偈曰
緬甸雖有大金塔支
那更有大銅鐘而者
皆為歷史物神鐘失
而復浮鳴。

# 116

## Viewing the relics at Ta Chung[6] Monastery

The Master viewed the eighty-four-thousand-pound bronze bell, which was cast by the Monk Yao Kuang Hsiao during the Ming Dynasty. It is several stories in height. Its crown is seven feet high, and it is fourteen feet in diameter. The entire *Avatamsaka (Flower Adornment) Sutra* is cast on the outside, and the *Dharma Flower Sutra* and the Tsun Sheng (Noble and Sublime) Mantra in their entirety are cast on the inside. The *Vajra Sutra* is cast on the lip, and on the crown, the Shurangama Mantra. It was offered by the Yung Le Emperor for the sake of crossing over his mother.

The gatha says:

> Although in Burma one can see
>     the magnificent Golden Stupa,
> The colossal Bronze Bell of China is
>     even greater yet.
> Both of these are renowned
>     historical objects.
> The cherished bell has now been lost,
>     but it will ring again.

---

6. "Great Bell"

回城南龍泉寺住
五月圍亂益熾以扶
清滅洋為辭各教日
使書記德公使太后
縱之至十七日下詔
與各國宣戰京大亂
六月天津失七月聯
軍陷北京時王公大
臣住龍泉者乃勸公
偕伊等随尾驛西行
宣化偈曰
清運將末南義和八
國聯軍入冠魔逼逼
太后長安去擁護聖
駕有頭阮。

# 117

## Returning to Ch'eng Nan[7] and staying at Lung Ch'üan[8] Monastery

By the fifth lunar month, the Boxer Rebellion had intensified. Their motto was "Support the Ch'ing Dynasty, and eliminate the foreigners." The Empress Dowager had condoned the assassination of the secretary of the Japanese Consulate and the German Ambassador. On the seventeenth of the month, war was declared on the foreign powers by imperial mandate. The capital was in tumult. The following month, T'ien Tsin was lost, and a month later Peking fell to the allied troops. During that time, the princes and ministers who were staying at Lung Ch'üan (Dragon Spring) Monastery urged the Master to join the Imperial Retinue in its flight west.

The gatha says:

> On the verge of ruin was old Ch'ing Dynasty,
>     as the Boxers were embattled.
> The allied armies of eight different countries
>     invaded like plundering demons.
> The Empress Dowager in dire straits
>     fled to Ch'ang An in the west.
> Protecting their royal majesties
>     was a man of ascetic practice.

---

7. "Southern City"
8. "Dragon Spring"

離北京赴長安
日夜兼程艱苦萬狀。
行至阜平縣始聞甘
肅岑春煊勤王兵至。
護駕出長城入山西
雁門關有雲門寺一
老僧已一百二十四
歲帝賜黃綾及建坊
又西行至平陽遍地
饑荒
宣化偈曰
一人有慶兆民賴萬
姓無辜多倒懸車駕
西行親經歷遍地饑
荒太可憐。

# 118

## Leaving Peking and heading towards Ch'ang An

Day and night, the forced march continued, despite the many difficulties and bitter sufferings. As they reached Fu P'ing County, the soldiers of Governor Ts'en Ch'un Hsüan of Kansu Province could be heard approaching to accompany the Monarch. They escorted their majesties past the Great Wall. After entering Yen Men (Wild Geese) Pass, Shanhsi Province, the Emperor met a one-hundred-twenty-four-year-old monk in Yün Men (Cloud Gate) Monastery, upon whom he bestowed some fine yellow robe-cloth. He also ordered the construction of an arch. The western march continued, and upon reaching P'ing Yang, they found that famine was widespread.

The gatha says:

> If a single leader enjoys good fortune,
>    all the people can rely on him.
> The common people were not at fault,
>    but still were suffering severely.
> When their majesties fled to the west,
>    they themselves experienced
> The serious famine which prevailed –
>    it was just too pitiful!

祈甘露雨息災
民以芋薯葉進帝后
食甘之至西安帝住
撫院有人食死屍者
諭葬之四城設八施
飯廠大小村鎮点然
換台岺春煌請公至
卧龍寺祈禱雪雨息
旱灾畢東霞雷住公
以罷煩甚潛去
宣化偈曰
治世犬勝乱世人遭次
頻沛頌忠臣遍地荒
旱民飢饉撫台請公
禱甘霖。

# 119

## Praying for the sweet dew of rain to avert disaster

The local people offered taro and potato leaves for the Emperor and Empress to eat, which their majesties found quite good. At Hsi An, the Emperor stayed at the Provincial Governor's headquarters. During this period, people were so hungry that they were eating corpses, so a prohibatory edict was issued. Eight rice-lines were set up in the urban areas, in addition to those set up in the big and small towns and the outlying areas. Governor Ts'en Ch'un Hsüan asked the Master to go to Wo Lung (Reclining Dragon) Monastery to offer prayers for snow or rain to end the drought. At the conclusion of the prayers, Abbot Tung Hsia requested that the Master remain, but because of the clamor and din, the Master secretly left.

The gatha says:

> One would rather be a dog during peaceful times
>     than a person during times of chaos.
> In the midst of roiling confusion and disorder
>     appeared a loyal minister.
> As the serious drought intensified,
>     with the cropless masses starving,
> The Provincial Governor asked the Master to pray
>     for a lasting sweet rain.

嘉五台獅子巖
十月上終南山嘉五
台獅子巖結茅地此
靜為杜外擾計改號
「盧雪山冬水化積雪
為飲摧野菜為食山
中有本昌住破石山
妙蓮住閣帝廟道明
住五華洞妙圓修圓。
青山分住後山
宣化偈曰
萬里終南隱聖賢。
千比丘聚長安公今
更名居獅洞專心致
志苦修參。

# 120

## Staying in Lion Cavern at Chia Wu T'ai Mountain

In the tenth lunar month, the Master climbed the Chung Nan Mountains to live in the wilds and stayed at the Lion Cavern of Chia Wu T'ai Mountain. The area was remote and still, and to avoid the annoyance of visitors, the Master changed his name to Hsü Yün (Empty Cloud). Since there was no water on the mountain, he melted snow to drink and gathered wild plants to eat. In the vicinity, Dharma Master Pen Ch'ang (Original Brilliance) was living on P'o Shih (Broken Rock) Mountain. Dharma Master Miao Lien (Wonderful Lotus) was dwelling at the Kuan Ti Temple. Dharma Master Tao Ming (Bright Way) was staying in Wu Hua (Five Flower) Cave. Also, Dharma Masters Miao Yüan (Wonderfully Complete), Hsiu Yüan (Complete Cultivation), and Ch'ing Shan (Blue Mountain), lived on different parts of the mountain in back.

The gatha says:

Ten thousand miles away,
    sequestered in Chung Nan, are the Worthy Sages,
While several hundreds of thousands of bhikshus
    in Ch'ang An gathered together.
The Master changed his name
    and took up residence in the Lion Cavern.
With single-minded concentration he
    practiced austerities and dhyana.

自耕自食自修
青山師湘人眾尊之。
兵公住戴近來徒自
種了庵三月復戌月
霞了庵三師至詫曰
戒年不知你消息竟
睡在這裏公笑曰這
裏且置如何是那裏
報吃芋畢住破石山
云法老戲煩欽某此。
宣化偈曰
化城引月渡戒師翠
微山上相地回公謂
無薬向白虎多山少
吉凶果然。

# 121

## Personally ploughing, personally eating, and personally cultivating

Dharma Master Ch'ing Shan (Blue Mountain) was a native of Hu Nan Province, and those in the mountains all respected him. Since he lived relatively close to the Master, they were naturally in contact. The Master planted his own vegetables. In the eighth lunar month of the following year, Dharma Masters Fu Ch'eng (Restored to Success), Yüeh Hsia (Moon Mist), and Liao Ch'en (Finished with the Dust) arrived. They were all surprised and said to the Master, "We had no news of you for several years. We never expected that you'd be sleeping *here*!" The Master laughed and said, "Never mind about here; where is *there*?!" After a meal of taro, the Master joined the group and stayed at P'o Shih (Broken Rock) Mountain. It was said that Elder Master Fa Jen (Dharma Patience) had been troubled lately and wanted to come to the area.

The gatha says:

> The Transformation City enticed
> > Dharma Masters "Moon Mist" and Fu Ch'eng,
> Who congregated
> > on this stretch of green mountain area.
> But the Master said it lacked support
> > since it faced a white tiger[9].
> Quite adverse and not propitious
> > – the result was just that way.

---

[9.] A term used in geomancy.

行路中堕雪窟

冬至青山老人嘱赴
長安市物返道大雪。
上山至新茅蓬石壁
懸崖間随雪窟中大
難。近棚一全上人來
救衣內外湿将夜恐
雪封山連夜撥雪歸。
詣青師見公粮狼嗞
不濟笑領之返度歳。
宣化偈曰
為人服務隨雪窟返
被呵嗞不濟徒徒勞
任怨任道遠證聖証
果証祖師。

# 122

## Falling into a snow cavity while walking

During the winter, the Master called on the Venerable Master Ch'ing Shan (Blue Mountain), who asked him to go to Ch'ang An for supplies. On the way back, the Master encountered a blizzard as he ascended the mountain. Nearing the new hut, he walked off an overhanging precipice and fell into a snow crevice. His loud hollering brought Dharma Master Yi Ch'üan (Oneness) from a nearby hut to his rescue. The Master's clothing was drenched and night was falling, but fearing that the snow would make the mountain inaccessible, he kept going on through the night. He finally reached Dharma Master Ch'ing Shan's hut, despite the snow. When Dharma Master Ch'ing Shan saw the Master's disheveled appearance, he laughed and told the latter he was useless. The Master smiled and returned to his hut to pass the New Year.

The gatha says:

> When the Master was doing someone a favor,
>    he fell into a snowy hollow.
> Upon his return, he was laughed at and mocked
>    as being a useless monk.
> He tolerated toil and criticism
>    – the road of his mission was long.
> He was certified to the fruition of Sagehood,
>    proving himself a Patriarch.

入定半月已兩年

辛丑六月十二歲法忍
老人率眾至後興土
人沙訟敗回南蓋風
水故也歲盡一日煮
芋待熟趺坐定去壬
寅六三鄰棚漫成師
見虎蹟徧滿入見公
定以磬開靜問已食
否

宣化偈曰　芋在釜
中度已熟啟視寧長
寸諳詩入定竟半月
煮雪煮芋飽笑乎。

# 123

## Entering samadhi for two weeks in two years

In the Master's sixty-second year, the Venerable Master Fa Jen (Dharma Patience) arrived with his following. He was soon involved in a civil suit, which he lost before returning south. All of this had something to do with the geomantic conditions of the area. The year was nearing its end. One day, while waiting for his taro to cook, Master Yün sat in the lotus posture and entered samadhi. The next year, Dharma Master Fu Ch'eng and others in neighboring huts were surprised to see that the Master had not come out to exchange New Year's greetings. They saw tiger tracks around his hut, and when they entered saw that the Master was in samadhi. Striking a small bell, they aroused him and politely asked if he had eaten yet.

The gatha says:

> The cooking taro in the pot
> > was already more than done.
> When the pot was opened, the taro inside
> > had grown an inch of mould!
> He had been in samadhi for half a month.
> > The others were taken aback.
> Drinking snow and cooking taro,
> > he was perfectly content.

厭酬答乃宵遁

復師去後遊遍僧俗。皆來觀拜公厭酬答。乃宵遁一肩衣單。又向萬里無寸草盧去。先至太白山居岩洞中。不久戒塵師蹤跡至。相約朝峨嵋山觀佛光興雞山無異夜看萬盞明燈興五台同。

宣化偈曰　錫气寶殿
裡真應年逾耳順領
袖僧宗門知識參学
飽歡曲教日又登程。

# 124

## Weary of visitors, leaving by night

After Dharma Master Fu and the others had left, bhikshus and laypeople from far and near began coming to call on and bow to the Master. He soon became weary of receiving so many visitors, and so one evening, shouldering his clothes bag, he left for the distant wilderness where there is not even one blade of grass. Initially he went to T'ai Pai (Great White) Mountain and lived in a chasm, but it wasn't long before Dharma Master Chieh Ch'en (Guarding Against the Dust) arrived, following the Master's footprints. They decided to go together on a pilgrimage to O-Mei Mountain. There the Buddha lights which the Master saw did not differ from the ones he had seen on Chi Tsu (Chicken Foot) Mountain. At night he observed a brilliance as bright as ten thousand lamps, similar to what he had seen on Wu T'ai (Five Peaks) Mountain.

The gatha says:

> In the Jeweled Palace paved with tin tiles,
>> he bowed to the One Truly Worthy of Offerings.
> The Master, whose age by now exceeded sixty years,
>> had become a leading Sanghan.
> As a well-known Advisor of the Ch'an School
>> his learning and practice were complete.
> He stayed happily there for a few days,
>> and then was on his way.

缆断流急堕水

下山循洗象池。大峨
寺长老坪昆卢啟峡
江县抵银村遁流沙
河早至午候船登以
皆登公讓戒師登以
衣單逝上公数登缆
急断流滾急公以石
子攀船弦舟人多側
即覆公不動浸暮。
宣化偶曰
攀船涉流度苦厄衣
温足破血柒河晒経
闽逢天寒雨旅唐不
留僧伽耶。

# 125

## Falling into a swift current when a rope breaks

Descending from the mountains, they passed by Hsi Hsiang (Washing Elephant) Lake, Ta-O (Great Mountain) Monastery, Chang Lao (Old Age) Plain, Vairochana Hall and through Hsia Chiang (Gorge) Prefecture. Upon arriving at Yin (Silver) Village, where they were to cross a river, they waited from morning till afternoon before the ferry finally arrived. Everyone had boarded, and the Master deferred to Dharma Master Chieh Ch'en, who boarded first. Handing the latter his bag, the Master was about to board when the rope suddenly broke. The current was swift, so the Master caught the gunwale of the boat with his right hand. Since the boat was overloaded, any slightest imbalance would have caused it to capsize. Therefore, the Master did not move, but remained in the water till the end of the day.

The gatha says:

> Grasping the boat afloat in the flow,
>     he crossed over suffering and misery.
> His clothes were drenched, his feet were cut,
>     and his blood stained the river.
> Arriving finally at Shai Ching Pass,
>     where it was cold and raining,
> They went to an inn, but had to stay out in the cold,
>     for Sanghans were not accepted.

拒掛單宿戲臺下

衢外有廟僅一僧住。
求宿不納令宿門外
戲臺底地潮衣濕天
寒膚冷向僧買禾草
拖來兩把濕杆燒之
不著思之與戒師坐
而待旦買香齋把食
而充飢忍著是痛仍
魁向前邁進也。
宣化偈曰
火燄山上放紅光金
沙江裏一毛黃晉賢
大士多奇妙觀音音
薩聖蹟彰。

# 126

## Bowing, being refused lodging, and spending the night under a stage

There was a temple a little ways from the street where only one bhikshu was dwelling, but he refused their request for lodging. They had to spend the night outdoors underneath a stage. The ground was damp and their clothes were wet. The freezing rain continued and the Master shivered. They purchased some straw from the monk in the temple, who gave them two wet bundles which wouldn't burn. The Master sat patiently with Dharma Master Chieh Ch'en until dawn, at which time they bought buckwheat groats to eat. The Master endured walking on his painful feet, still managing to make progress on their pilgrimage.

The gatha says:

> Fire burning in the mountain emitted
>     a red, glowing light.
> The color of the Golden Sand river
>     is a solid yellow.
> The Great Bodhisattva Samantabhadra[10]
>     is very rare and wondrous,
> And Avalokiteshvara Bodhisattva's
>     sagely relics were seen.

---

[10.] Universal Worthy

福興寺公閉關
朝鶴呈山樹下宿澹
閱石門內魚整驚聖
日金頂進香畢澹念
佛祖道場衰敗如斯。
全滇僧規隨落潺顏
結茅接眾又被子孫
寺廟所藜濘嘆護赴昆
明叅寬慈當住福興
閉關戒師護慶戒
宣化偈曰
癸卯公年六十四迎
祥故生有雄鶴惺極
財門傷同類公教念
佛接三皈。

# 127

## Going into seclusion at Fu Hsing[11] Monastery

While making a pilgrimage to Chicken Foot Mountain, they spent the night under a tree, and the following morning, heard the sound of the wooden fish and large bell inside the stone gate. The next day, after offering incense on Golden Summit, the Master thought of how this Way-place of the Buddhas and Patriarchs had degenerated to its present state, and about the neglect of the Sangha's moral rules in all Yunnan Province. He wanted to make a vow to live in a hut and receive traveling Sanghans, but was prevented from doing so by the hereditary monastic system. The Master sighed tearfully and went on to K'un Ming. At the request of Upasaka Ts'en K'uan Ts'e, the Master stayed at Fu Hsing (Fortune and Prosperity) Monastery, where he went into seclusion with the aid of Dharma Master Chieh Ch'en and passed the New Year.

The gatha says:

> The Master's age was sixty-four years
> in the cyclical year Kuei Mao.[12]
> Liberated at Ying Hsiang[13]Temple
> there was a dauntless cock
> Whose nature was fond of fighting,
> and it injured those of its kind.
> The Master taught it to be mindful of the Buddha,
> and it received the Three Refuges.

---

[11.] "Fortune and Prosperity"
[12.] 1903 A.D.
[13.] Welcoming Good Luck

皈依後念佛往生

浚不鬥獨棲樹不傷
虫不與不食念佛立
化公銘曰。好鬥成性
此雞雄傷冠拔羽血
流紅知畏奉戒狂心
歇素食孤棲不害虫。
兩目瞻仰黃金相念
佛喔喔何淩容旋繞
三撲奮然化眾生興
佛將無同。
宣化偈曰　雄雞念佛
尚往生吾人豈可不猜
勤念茲在茲不間斷一
心不亂悟無生。

# 128

## After a cock takes refuge, it is mindful of the Buddha, and goes off to rebirth

After that, the cock no longer fought, but perched alone in a tree. It did not harm insects, and so if no one gave it food, it did not eat. One day, it died standing up, reciting the Buddha's name. The Master then wrote the following verse:

> To be fond of fighting was the disposition
> of this dauntless cock,
> Which injured fowl, pulling out their plumes,
> making their red blood flow.
> But, knowing fear, it took the precepts;
> thereupon, its mad mind stopped.
> Roosting alone and a vegetarian,
> it no longer injured insects.
> Its eyes would gaze up and contemplate
> the yellow-golden images,
> While it crowed reciting the Buddha's name
> without any difficulty.
> After circling around and bowing three full bows,
> it peacefully passed away.
> What difference can be found
> between beings and the Buddhas?

The gatha says:

> Even the dauntless cock recited "Buddha,"
> and then went off to rebirth,
> So how can we who are people
> afford not to be diligent?
> Being ever mindful,
> ever reciting without interruption,
> Single-minded, without confusion,
> one enlightens to non-production.

鉢盂庵移巨石

公被各檀越懇請出
閱諸經法延遍滇境
李提督福興面公曰
崇聖寺公曰吾願在
鶴山閒掛單搜盡
令賓川辨理覓得
孟庵畱草搭銀而門
右有巨石高等寬等
主白馬不詳禪伽藍
辛僧移丟
宣化偶曰　拾工募
石難移公祈護法助
神力怪石搬家很搭
異威德威挃太妙寺

# 129

## Removing a huge rock at Po Yü[14] Temple

Entreated by various protectors of the Dharma to end his seclusion and explain Sutras, the Master took part in many Dharma assemblies around Yunnan Province. After that, General Li Fu Hsing requested that the Master stay at Ch'ung Sheng (Honoring Sages) Monastery. The Master replied, "I have made a vow to set up a place on Chicken Foot Mountain to receive traveling Sanghans." The General thereupon ordered Pin Ch'uan to make a search. He found Po Yü (Bowl) Temple as a possible site where visiting Sanghans could be accomodated, but to the right of the temple was a large rock measuring eight feet tall and six feet wide. Since it was dominated by a white tiger[15], it was quite inauspicious. The Master prayed to the Sangharama Spirits and led a group of bhikshus in moving the rock away.

The gatha says:

> Over a hundred workers who were hired
>     could not budge the rock.
> The Master prayed to the Dharma-protecting Spirits
>     to lend their power.
> When the peculiar stone was moved away,
>     everyone said, "How strange!"
> His abundant virtue evoked a response
>     – miraculous indeed!

---

14. "Bowl"
15. A term used in geomancy; see #121

路遇禪僧苦修道

公以修寺。急於募化。
乃下山行至一和木樹。
遇一僧修路禮不答。
晚對坐次晨作飯公
為燒火飯熟不招呼。
取箸食畢僧荷鋤公
負箕同修路十餘日
未造一語相安同處
止與皆如是。
宣化偈曰
捕萃數百路難行楚
僧禪修賴地平苦行
教十年不退高矣休
哉嘆奇全。

# 130

## Meeting Dharma Master Ch'an Hsiu[16] who cultivated austerities

The Master immediately went to raise the money required to repair the broken-down temple. As he descended the mountain, upon reaching Ho Mu tree, he met a monk who was repairing the road. The Master bowed, but the monk did not respond. In the evening, they sat facing each other, and the next morning, the monk cooked some rice while the Master stoked the fire. When it was ready, the monk did not tell him to eat, but the Master did so anyway. The monk then shouldered his hoe and the Master carried the basket. They worked together in that way for more than ten days without exchanging a single word. Thus, in mutual harmony, they toiled and rested together.

The gatha says:

> Rough and craggy for several hundred miles,
>     the road was hard to travel.
> The monk Ch'an Hsiu
>     vowed to make it passable,
> So he bitterly toiled for several decades,
>     and never once retreated.
> Eminent indeed was Hsiu!
>     The Master sighed at this strange encounter.

---

16. "Ch'an Cultivation"

對月論禪皆大笑

一夕月明龐公跌
坐大石上僧悄至背
後大喝曰在此做甚
龐公徐啟目緩應曰
看月僧曰月在何處
公曰大好霞光僧曰
往多魚目真雞辨休
認虹霓是彩霞公曰
光含萬象氣今古不
屬陰陽純障遮

宣化偈曰
彼此大笑一貫通深夜
請回睡矇矓金山得一
休歇塵修早地不施功

# 131

## Discussing Ch'an in terms of the moon: both had a good laugh

Once, when the moonlit evening was as bright as day, the Master sat in meditation with crossed legs on a large rock. The monk silently approached from behind and shouted, "What are you doing here?!" The Master slowly opened his eyes, and unhurriedly replied "I'm looking at the moon." The monk then said, "Where is the moon?" The Master answered, "In its magnificent glowing light." The monk said:

> Finding the pearls among fish eyes
>     is difficult to do.
> Do not mistake the rainbow
>     for the spectrum of true light.

The Master then replied:

> The light embraces the ten thousand things
>     but has no past or present.
> Not defined by yin or yang,
>     all obstructions are gone.

The gatha says:

> This and that were strung through;
>     the two of them shared a hearty laugh,
>     and everything was penetrated.
> Late at night, he asked the Master
>     to return and take his rest.
> Back at Gold Mountain,
>     he attained the One – the place of true rest.
> All day long he leveled the ground
>     and did not boast of his work.

為和尚念經施食

往騰衝住湘會館行
單來卸肓服孝者數
人叩禮云請大師念
經公答非應赴經僧
孝子云為你們和尚
念經飯人曰大師要
玄來者為吳太史曾
孫太史乃善人臨終
謂為僧有高僧來度
宣化偈曰
念經施食滿來復圓
邑官仲頎做徒悲苗
騰越芳緣急璕躍樂
捐鉅款翰

**132**

## Reciting sutras and bestowing food
## upon a monk

The Master then left for T'eng Ch'ung, where he stayed in the Hunan Provincial Association Hall. Before he could put down his bag, however, several mourners bowed and said, "We respectfully request that the Venerable Master recite Sutras for the deceased." The Master told them that he was not a monk who had come to recite Sutras. A mourner then said, "Surely you can recite Sutras for a fellow monk!" A man from the Association said, "The Venerable Master ought to go with them. These people are the grandsons of the Imperial Historian Wu, who was a beneficent man. Just before his death, he said that he wished to become a member of the Sangha, and that an eminent monk would soon arrive to rescue him."

The gatha says:

Reciting Sutras and bestowing food
        were rites well attended.
The entire town, officials and gentry,
        wished to become disciples.
They entreated him to stay in T'eng Yüeh,
        but subscriptions were more important,
So in their joy, they happily pledged
        substantial contributions.

弘法讲经擅城

回庵备粮传戒弘法
受瘴病柳洞化定如
师至缅高万邪接待
神金塔搭船赴擅城
登岸被检验有疫隔
离于山人皆放留公
以药毒之不死浮闻
人救至极乐寺病瘳
讲妙法莲华经
宣化偈曰
表曹存心颇狠毒
本来死欲剖腹岂意
大德佛呵护雄服毒
刹有若无

# 133

## Propagating the Dharma and explaining the sutras in Penang

The Master returned to the monastery with provisions. The Precepts were transmitted, and the Dharma flourished. Later he contracted malaria, and at Liu Tung (Willow Cave), instructed Dharma Master Ting Ju (Still Suchness). Proceeding on to Burma, he was received by Upasaka Kao Wan Pang. After paying his respects to the Golden Stupa, he took passage to Penang by boat. Passing through the health inspection upon disembarking, all of the passengers were quarantined on a distant hill. Although everyone was subsequently released, the Master was left to die from the poisoned medicine he had been given. His life was saved by a native of Fukien Province. The Master then went to Chi Le (Ultimate Bliss) Monastery, where he recuperated, and lectured on the *Wonderful Dharma Lotus Flower Sutra*.

The gatha says:

> The barbarious doctor harbored in his heart
>     the poison of strong hatred;
> Even when a patient had not yet died,
>     he wanted to cut open his stomach.
> But this Greatly Virtuous One
>     the Buddhas will protect,
> So although the Master swallowed the poison,
>     it was as if not there.

回國挽救寺難
演全體僧來電云政
府提寺產寄禪約回
國共國挽救丙午六
十七歲春回國船經
台參觀靈泉寺至日
參觀各地佛寺時中
日暗交惡兩國僧人
六不許自由活動三
月回國抵滬上
宣化偈曰
妙老回國釋諸經法
華藥師繼闡明吉隆
靈山詩楞伽前後敏
依萬餘名。

# 134

## Returning to China to save the monasteries

The Master received a telegram from the Yunnan Province Sangha Association, which said that the government was seizing monastery property. Dharma Master Chi Ch'an urged the Master to return to China where the problem could be collectively resolved. In the spring of 1906, the Master's sixty-seventh year, he departed for China. When the ship stopped at Taiwan, he visited Ling Ch'uan (Magic Spring) Monastery, and later in Japan, visited various Buddhist temples. At that time, communications between China and Japan were worsening, and members of the Sangha in both countries were forbidden freedom of movement. In the third lunar month, the Master returned to his country, arriving at Shanghai.

The gatha says:

> The Venerable Miao returned to China
> and urged him to lecture Sutras.
> The *Dharma Flower* and *Medicine Master* sutras
> he successively expounded clearly.
> At Ling Shan (Magic Mountain) Temple in
> Kuala Lumpur, he explained the *Lankavatara*.
> Altogether more than ten thousand people
> took refuge with the Master.

一同進京請願

興佛教會代表齊禪師等同進京請願抵京住賢良寺僧錄司。法安龍泉寺道興觀音寺覺光諸師等視自招待。備極優隆彼此共商又何進行挽救策略此時善那公等。佛教不知伊于胡底。宣化偈曰

三武滅佛佛不滅。再護教教復興進京。諸願跋涉苦晶浮功勳傳古今。

城隍

永定門

## 135

## Arriving in the capital to join a group in petitioning the government

The Master, Dharma Master Chi Ch'an, and the other representatives of the Buddhist Association, entered the capital to present their petition to the government. Upon arriving, they stayed at Hsien Liang (Good and Worthy) Monastery. The official Head of Sangha Affairs, Dharma Master Fa An of Lung Ch'üan (Dragon Springs) Monastery, Dharma Master Tao Hsing of Kuan Yin Temple, along with Dharma Master Chüeh Kuang and others personally welcomed the Master, lavishly supplying him with all manner of provisions. All the Masters discussed among themselves how to rectify the situation and make plans for restoration. Had it not been for the efforts of the Master and the others, who knows what would have happened to Buddhism?

The gatha says:

> Three Wu emperors persecuted the Buddhists,
>     but Buddhism did not die.
> The Teaching was protected
>     and flourished once again.
> Going to the capital to present their petition,
>     they traveled a difficult path.
> The story of their glorious merit
>     has come down from past to present.

王公宰官護法

時齋觀王善者請公為其太福晉說戒法。復有庚子歲公隨鸞駕護帝后西行時。各王公大臣舊相知多來探視籌劃上奏諸事宜得各護法幫助甚力諸事順利進行。奏上旋奉上諭傳。宣化偈曰

琉璃大王戒釋種頻婆娑羅請目連來視王子為護法遂心滿頌奉諭遵。

# 136

## Receiving protection for the Dharma from princes, dukes, officials and the emperor

At that time, Prince Su Shan Ch'i requested that the Master explain appropriate precepts to his wife. Moreover, the princes, dukes, and ministers whom the Master had met while accompanying the Emperor and Empress and the Imperial Caravan during its westward flight in 1900[17] lent their influence in the formal presentation of the petition. Because of the profound power of the aid given by the Dharma Protectors, all went smoothly, and as a result, a prohibatory edict was proclaimed.

The gatha says:

> The great and powerful Crystal King
>    demolished the Shakyan clan.
> And the King called Bimbisara
>    had entreated Maudgalyayana.
> At this time, there was Prince Su Shan Ch'i,
>    who was also a protector of the Dharma.
> In accord with their wishes,
>    an Imperial edict was proclaimed.

---

[17.] See #118.

敕封佛慈洪法大師回山
欽賜龍藏鑾駕全幅。
敕命方丈御賜紫衣
鉢具玉印錫杖如意
敕封住持盧雲佛慈
洪法大師之諭奉旨
回山傳戒護國佑民。
內務府大臣傳知盧
雲謹領各件回山永
鎮山門善為布教官
民一体虔奉加意保
護毋得輕褻此諭
宣化偈曰　佛慈洪法
尊讀願志已伸奉旨回
祝聖布教化群倫。

# 137

## Being conferred the title "Vast Dharma of the Buddha's Compassion" and returning to the mountain

The Emperor then bestowed upon the Master a set of Imperial Tripitaka, a complete Imperial carriage, as well as a purple robe, a bowl, a jade seal, a tin staff, and an as-you-will sceptre.

"The Venerable Abbot Hsü Yün is hereby granted the title 'The Great Master Vast Dharma of the Buddha's Compassion,' and it is hereby decreed that he is entrusted with returning to the mountain to transmit the precepts for the protection of the country and its people. The Secretary of the Interior is hereby instructed to inform the Venerable Abbot Hsü Yün of this edict, which provides that he receive the gifts and return to the mountain, where he can be ever protective of its monasteries, and continue to make known the Teachings. The public officials and citizens of the area should sincerely implement and protect this proclamation. Disregard for it will not be tolerated."

The gatha says:

> The petition of the Honored One,
>     Vast Dharma of the Buddha's Compassion,
> Was now accepted.
> By Imperial edict he returned to
>     Chu Sheng Mountain
> To spread the teachings and
>     transform all classes of beings.

戒源和尚妙老示寂

丁未六十八歲春運
任回山抵廈接鼓山
電云妙蓮老人於正
月在龜山圓寂公乘
程回山建塔連日滂
沱四月十日進塔八
日晴十日官仲士庶
絡繹於道供品百桌
上供念變食真言時
忽起旋風吹至空中塔放
霞光　宣化偈曰
霞光貫塔透九霄瞻仰
稽嘆妙公高供畢回寺
滂沱兩咸應道交不錯毫

# 138

## Venerating Venerable Miao, source of the precepts master, upon his entering the stillness

The Master was sixty-eight in 1907. Transporting the Tripitaka back to the mountain, he reached Amoy in the spring, where he received a telegram from Ku Shan (Drum Mountain) informing him that the Venerable Miao Lien (Wonderful Lotus) had passed away on Kuei Shan Mountain in the first month of the year. The Master immediately left for the mountain to set up the stupa. It rained heavily day after day. On the tenth day of the fourth lunar month, a stupa was completed, and on the eighth of the following month, the weather was clear. On the tenth, the public officials, scholars and common people took to the roads in a continuous stream to the mountain. There were one hundred tables of offerings, and during the recitation of the food-transforming mantra, a sudden whirlwind arose and lifted aloft the offerings. A multi-colored light was seen coming from the stupa.

The gatha says:

> Rainbow light came forth from the stupa
>     penetrating to the Ninth Heaven.
> All looked up with sounds of praise
>     for the eminent Master Miao.
> When the offering was over, he returned to the
>     temple, pelted by torrents of rain.
> The Way and response are intertwined
>     and not off by a hair.

洋人信佛供僧

奉藏及妙公靈骨至
檳城迎者數千人供
念宴食真言旋風渡
起霞光如前妙公以
建寺結緣秘行難思
公誦心經轉船赴泰
有一英人來訪說國
語談次乃知是英駐
滇使助洋三千
宣化偈曰
化行中外度洋人樂
助輪將三千銀若非
至德烏如是因緣恩
及獸與禽。

# 139

## Meeting a Westerner who believes in the Buddha and makes an offering to the Sangha

The Master proceeded on to Penang, Malaysia, with the Imperial Tripitaka, and the relics of the Venerable Miao. There were several thousand people who welcomed him upon arrival. During the ceremonies, when the food-transforming mantra was being recited, a whirlwind again arose, and multi-colored light was seen as before. The Venerable Master Miao had tied up conditions by establishing temples, and the profundity of his secret practices was inconceivable indeed. The Master expounded on the *Heart Sutra*, and then traveled by boat to Thailand. On board was an Englishman who spoke Chinese with the Master. The man turned out to be the British consul stationed in Yunnan Province. He contributed $3,000.

The gatha says:

> Teaching and practicing in China and abroad,
>     he also converted a Westerner,
> Who gladly aided with his own contribution
>     of three thousand dollars in silver.
> If the Master's virtue had not been supreme,
>     how could this event have happened?
> His affinities and kindness extended
>     to the birds and beasts as well.

安然禪定九日
一日安然入定經九
日哄動遥京國王大
臣男女善信咸來羅
拜出定誦經畢王請
至宮中誦經畢王請
養東誠皈依官伸士
庶皈依者數千人鳴
呼人皆好奇異未定
不識已定乃知
宣化偈曰
圓王皈依信三寶。大
匡頂礼學一乘士人
崇拜俏無上庶民同
化入空門

# 140

## Being absorbed in dhyana samadhi for nine days

One day, the Master entered the stillness of dhyana samadhi, and nine days passed. The capital city of Thailand was greatly aroused because of this. The King and his ministers, as well as the faithful men and women, all came to bow to the Master. After the Master came out of samadhi, and after he had lectured a Sutra, the King requested that the Master recite Sutras in his court. There were one hundred different offerings, and many sincere people took refuge, including public officials and gentry, several thousand in all. Ah, everyone is fond of strange feats. Nobody recognized him before he entered samadhi; only after he entered samadhi did they know!

The gatha says:

> The Emperor himself took refuge with
>     and believed in the Triple Jewel.
> His ministers all bowed in reverence to
>     and studied the Single Vehicle.
> The literati paid their respects
>     and practiced the unsurpassed.
> The masses were transformed together,
>     and entered the door of emptiness.

麻瘋病迦葉入夢

定後足染麻瘋徧全
身枯木不能執著食
人餵眼不見口難言。
醫無效放下惟衣領
維湼槃無人知為念。
因采波下衲迦葉尊
者加被妙圓師在側。
取茶褊迦葉脈入夢。
見尊者云衣缽不離。
枕之愈。

宣化偈曰　睏睡忽汗
愈況疴寄語妙師求藥
阮木櫛夜明砂二味丹
求赤豆作粥合。

# 141

## Becoming paralyzed and seeing Mahakashyapa appear in a vision

After that samadhi experience, the Master's feet became numb, and as the numbness spread, his whole body withered. He couldn't even hold chopsticks, and he had to be fed by others. His sight was gone, and he experienced extreme difficulty in talking. The doctors who came were not effective. The Master had put everything down, however, except for a money order sewn into his collar about which no one else knew. He thought of the causes and results involved, and as his tears fell, he prayed to the Venerable Kashyapa for aid. Dharma Master Miao Yuan (Wonderous Perfection) was at the Master's side giving him tea, as he continued to beseech the Venerable Kashyapa. In a vision, the latter told the Master: "Bhikshu! Do not leave your robe and bowl – use them as a pillow, and you will be cured!"

The gatha says:

With internal disturbance and sudden sweat,
 his serious illness was cured.
A message was mouthed to Master Miao,
 to seek medicine from Hua T'ou[18].
A prescription consisting of Mu Chieh and
 Yeh Ming sifted together appeared;
Then, together with red beans, they were
 made into a gruel.

---

[18.] A brilliant surgeon who developed the art of acupuncture at the end of the Han Dynasty (3rd Century A.D.)

秦皇臣民拜送
病愈復請起信論攜
極樂寺派善信論月
來接秦皇及諸王大
臣護法善信皆來送
復送洞裡地三百頃。
行贈資歡甚鉅遷皇
公卿轉送極樂寺善
慶和高設樹彌廠公
偕二師在廠通年。
宣化偈曰
充寶道德有光輝圓
儒萬行無倫比義大
聖神儒推重信住行
向佛理微。

**142**

## Being seen off by the emperor, ministers, and people of Thailand

When the Master was cured, he continued to explain the *Shastra for the Awakening of Faith in the Mahayana*. Dharma Masters Shan Ch'in (Good Reverence) and Pao Yüeh (Jeweled Moon) were sent by Chi Le Monastery (Ultimate Bliss) in Penang to escort the Master there. The Thai King, princes, ministers, and faithful protectors of the Dharma all came to see him off. There were numerous donations, and the King himself gave three hundred *ch'ing*[19] of land at Tung Li. The Master then turned over the land to Chi Le Monastery, where Dharma Master Shan Ch'ing (Wholesome Rejoicing) was to set up a rubber factory. The Master passed the new year on the plantation with the other two Dharma Masters.

The gatha says:

> His full and genuine virtue in the Way
> shone with dazzling light.
> He practiced to perfection the ten thousand
> conduct–he was without equal.
> Beauty, greatness, sageliness, and spirituality
> are the qualities Confucianists extol.
> The positions of the Faiths, the Dwellings,
> the Practices, and the Transferences
> are subtle principles within Buddhism.

---

[19.] Approximately 4,500 acres.

檳城掩方便關

戊申公六十九歲春。
公偕善和尚慶老自
峨觀音閣乃至雪蘭
莪旋至怡保大小霹
靂參觀往極樂寺謁
起信論行願品信心
銘依者眾經畢。即閉
方便關暫停講倚禪
不會客在寺度歲。
宣化偈曰
熱鬧場中度春秋。
己耘人不自憂誠恐
後學隨此病公故示
現掩關修。

# 143

## Expediently entering seclusion at Penang

In the spring of 1908, the Master's sixty-ninth year, he traveled to Kuan Yin Temple in Selangor with the Venerable Master Shan Ch'ing (Wholesome Rejoicing) who was its founder. They visited the great and small Pi Li Caves at Ipoh, and the Master subsequently stayed at Chi Le (Ultimate Bliss) Monastery, where he lectured the *Shastra for the Awakening of Faith in the Mahayana* and the *Chapter on the Vows and Conduct of Universal Worthy*. Many faithful devotees took refuge. When the Sutra lectures were over, he expediently entered into seclusion and temporarily suspended further lecturing. Cultivating dhyana samadhi, he did not receive any guests, and spent New Year's at the monastery.

The gatha says:

> Toiling in the noisy fields
> > he spent many springs and autumns.
> He gave himself up to training people
> > and never worried on his own behalf.
> However, afraid that his pupils
> > would fall into this illness,[20]
> He purposely set an example of entering into
> > seclusion to step up his cultivation.

---

[20.] The illness of being overly involved in the hub-bub of noisy life and neglecting the cultivation of Ch'an.

奉龍藏回國寺

己酉七十歲公由檳
運經至仰光萬邦高
居士接至家月餘送
瓦城贈臥玉佛到新
衘寄觀音亭催馱馬
三百餘人馬同行載
連千銀經騰越下關
各地方均看迎送行
數十日甚平安

宣化偈曰

仰光護法高萬邦財
力二施非尋常堪嗟
末法人多障再如高
君立元無雙。

# 144

## Taking the Imperial Tripitaka back to the National Temple

In 1909, the Master's seventieth year, he traveled with the Imperial Tripitaka from Penang to Rangoon where he was received by Upasaka Kao Wan Pang at his home. The Master stayed there for over a month, and then was escorted by Upasaka Kao to Mandalay, where the latter donated a reclining jade Buddha. At Hsin Chieh, the Master enshrined the statue at Kuan Yin Pavilion, and later hired more than three hundred pack horses to carry the Tripitaka, along with men to lead them. Passing through T'eng Yüeh and Hsia Kuan, and at each place along the way, there were people to welcome and escort the caravan, which consisted of about a thousand men and horses. They traveled for several weeks, and their journey was very peaceful.

The gatha says:

> The Dharma protector from Rangoon,
>     layman Kao Wan Pang,
> Donated both his wealth and efforts
>     – how rare a man was this!
> Alas that in this sad Dharma-Ending Age,
>     people have many obstructions.
> You could not find another man like Kao.

牛求救屠政業
富抵騰越寓萬壽寺。
典提督張松林坐談。
忽来黃牛跪面前眼
重淚旋楊勝昌屠者
多人至公向牛曰汝
欲生須皈依三寶牛
点首為誦三皈依牛
主誓政業皈依長齋
軍門台為店傭。
宣化偈曰
以羊易牛宣王心恩
及禽獸政施仁孟軻
闹此千里至黃牛皈
依萬古新。

# 145

## Helping an ox gain deliverance, and a butcher changes profession

Reaching the town of T'eng Yüeh, the Master stayed in Wan Shou (Ten Thousand Years) Temple. One day, as he was sitting and talking with the Provincial Governor Chang Sung Lin, a yellow ox suddenly appeared. It knelt down before the Master, shedding tears. Following it was a butcher named Yang Sheng Ch'ang, and several others. The Master said to the ox, "If you wish to live, you must take refuge with the Triple Jewel." The ox nodded its head and was given the Three Refuges. The owner of the ox, the butcher, vowed to change his profession, took refuge, and became a vegetarian. The governor recommended him for a job in a store.

The gatha says:

> Substituting an ox for a sheep,
>     Emperor Hsüan showed a princely heart.
> With empathy reaching to even the birds and
>     beasts, he governed with humaneness.
> If Mencius had heard about this event,
>     he would have come a thousand miles.
> A yellow ox had taken refuge –
>     a rarity in ten thousand years!

龍迎經官接旨

進大理府時雷電交
作洱海波騰雲虹變
幻作奇景無雨至寺
行迎經大典安妥乃
大雨滂沱每日仍晴
咸謂洱海龍王迎經
時雲貴總督李經義
率官伸接旨迎藏
觀斯異嘆佛法無边

宣化偈曰

一路平安無滴雨
千軍浩蕩有瑞雲腕月
三十正香會歡騰萬
銀浮未曾

# 146

## Observing a dragon welcoming the Imperial Tripitaka, and public officials doing the same

Amidst lightning, crashes of thunder and great swells on Erh Hai Lake, they approached Ta Li Fu. The clouds and rainbows brought about unusual transformations of the scenery. No rain fell on the way to the monastery, but after a welcoming ceremony, when the Tripitaka was safe in the Great Hall, torrential rain fell. Afterwards, every day was clear, and it was said that the Dragon King of Erh Hai Lake was welcoming the Tripitaka. At this time, the Viceroy of Yunnan and Kueichow Provinces, Li Ching Yi, led a delegation of public officials who had received an Imperial order to welcome the Tripitaka. They personally witnessed the strange events described above, and marvelled at the boundlessness of the Buddhadharma.

The gatha says:

> The entire trip was very peaceful,
>      without a drop of rain.
> A host of thousands of people
>      was protected by auspicious clouds.
> On the thirtieth of the leap year month,
>      an incense ceremony was held.
> As the incense joyously rose, all in attendance
>      experienced something they never had before.

一念慈孙封書

庚戌七十一歲目前
年集提寺產及藏經
回山僧伽漸遵戒法。
提倡青年教育李帥
家眷皈依放葉僧釋
罪囚夏鼓山轉家信
兩封彈指五十年有
詩云。祝此一生清白
業云云之句
宣化偈曰
一念慈悲萬佛欽。六
度修成眾聖源九品
蓮花迎妙淨滿輪明
月照公岩。

# 147

## Having one thought of compassion and receiving two letters

The Master was seventy-one in 1910. Because of the prohibition of selling monastery property, and the arrival of the Tripitaka on the mountain, the Sangha gradually came to honor the moral precepts again. The Master continued to promote education for young monks. Viceroy Li and his whole family took refuge, and monks and others still in jail were released. In the summer, the Master received two letters from home, forwarded from Ku Shan (Drum Mountain). In what seemed like a finger snap, fifty years had passed. The Master wrote a poem, which reads in part:

> In this lifetime I have tried to purify my karma,
> So that no other affairs hang in my mind.

The gatha says:

> With a single thought of compassion,
>     Ten Thousand Buddhas smile.
> When the Six Perfections are completed,
>     that is the source of many Sages.
> All nine grades of lotus flower
>     usher in "Wonderful Purity,"
> As the wheel-like brightness of the full moon
>     shines down on the Master's mountain.

老栗樹開曇華

公應名僧伽。及檀越
請講楞嚴經。昇座說
法際。庭前老栗樹忽
湧開優缽曇華數十
朵大如盆形如芙蕖。
色五黃金含香吐蕊。
中空體潔威開敷月。
而不萎謝見者皆稱
奇異嘆未曾有。
宣化偈曰
老樹通靈獻妙供
童仰首望仙華僧伽
咸說奇華瑞檀越飯
敬勝菩提。

# 148

## Witnessing Udumbara flowers bloom
## on the old chestnut tree

The Master responded to an invitation by various members of the Sangha and benefactors to explain the *Shurangama Sutra*. When the Master had ascended his seat and was speaking the Dharma, the old chestnut tree in front of the hall suddenly blossomed, sending forth several tens of clusters of Udumbara flowers. They were big as basins and had the form of peonies, with a golden-yellow hue. Rare fragrance exuded from them; and they were empty in the middle, reflecting their purity of form. They bloomed lushly for several months and did not wither. Everyone who saw them pronounced it a marvel and exclaimed that there had never been anything like it before.


The gatha says:

>A little magic by the old tree
>>brought forth miraculous offerings,
>As the youngsters turned their heads to
>>gaze at the supernatural blooms.
>All the Sanghans together agreed
>>on the flowers' propitious rarity,
>While respectful donors took refuge
>>with sublime Bodhi.

續慧命傳佛戒

辛亥七十二歲公以
培植法器造就青年
僧材於春期傳授千佛
大戒於祝聖寺四方
求戒者恰滿千人於
五十三天內如法次
第僧事沙彌比丘菩
薩三壇大戒圓滿成
就新戒信受奉行

宣化偈曰
正法住世佛為師儀
末當依木叉尸公續
慧命傳寶戒吾儕法
身灘沭時

**149**

## Furthering the life of wisdom and transmitting the precepts

By the year 1911, at seventy-two, the Master, wishing to mould Dharma vessels by educating young Sanghans, transmitted the Great Precepts of the Thousand Buddhas in the spring, at Chu Sheng Monastery. There were exactly one thousand people in attendance who came from all over, filling the monastery to capacity. In accordance with the proper sequence and method of this ceremony, the three great Platforms of Shramanera, Bhikshu, and Bodhisattva Precepts were completed in fifty-three days. The newly-precepted faithfully received them and vowed to offer up their conduct.

The gatha says:

> When the Proper Dharma is in the world,
>     the Buddha is the Master.
> In Dharma Image and Ending Ages,
>     rely on the Pratimoksha.
> The Master extended the Life of Wisdom
>     and transmitted the precious Precepts,
> For this is when our Dharma bodies
>     are actually anointed.

健祖燈打禪七

公鑑祖道式微宗風
不振故傳戒而後即
舉行禪七。四十九日。
力倡宗風注重坐香
上殿過堂威儀慈祥
規約森嚴以期由戒
生定由定發慧使佛
祖心燈永照菩隆法
水常流盡未來際。
宣化偈曰
楞嚴大定妙總持三
摩禪那無所思者向
直指西來意狂心歇
廢即菩提。

**150**

## Continuing the lamp of the Patriarchs and holding a dhyana session

The Master saw that the Way of the Patriarchs was declining and that the tradition and repute of the dhyana school was shaky. In an attempt to revitalize the Ch'an school, after the transmission of the precepts a forty-nine day dhyana meditation session was convened, during which the proper demeanor while sitting, as well as during the ceremonies of the formal meal offering, was emphasized. Awesome comportment was stressed, as well as strict adherence to monastic rules. In time, from precepts grows samadhi, and from samadhi is developed wisdom. The Master caused the lamp of the Buddhas and Patriarchs to shine forever, and the Dharma water of the Bodhisattvas to overflow to the very bounds of the future.

The gatha says:

> In the Great Shurangama Concentration
>     is a miraculous dharani.
> Dhyana samadhi
>     is without mentation.
> If asked to point out directly
>     the meaning coming from the West,
> Just the place where the mad mind stops
>     is itself enlightenment.

根源協統毀佛寺
辛亥革命宣統遜位。
到處毀寺拆廟滅像。
逐僧滇省協統李根
源領導軍隊毀像拆
寺毅僧屠尼尤以公
乃窮和尚竟能深得
民心群眾擁護豈非
怪事故指名捕之禍
將不免危乎武
宣化偈曰
諸寺僧逃公不然如
屬業報何避焉以身
殉佛比丘志眾悅誠
服顧患難。

# 151

## Facing danger when Commander Ken Yüan begins to destroy Buddhist Monasteries

The Chinese Revolution started in 1911, and the last Manchu Emperor, Hsüan T'ung, abdicated the throne. Everywhere monasteries and temples were laid waste, images were destroyed, and members of the Sangha were expelled. The Yunnan Provincial Commander, Li Ken Yüan, led his infantry troops in the destruction of monasteries and statues, murdering bhikshus and butchering bhikshunis. That the Master, a poor monk, could profoundly win the heart of the common multitude and be venerated and protected by them, seemed very strange to Li. So, the commander ordered his arrest. A catastrophe was imminent – dangerous indeed!

The gatha says:

> All the monks of the monasteries fled,
>     but the Master did not do so.
> From one's own karmic retribution
>     how can one escape?
> To sacrifice one's body for the Buddha
>     is a bhikshu's aspiration.
> The masses took delight in complying with him
>     and willingly suffered hardships.

数语化凶为吉

协饶率兵驻志柱寺毁
金顶鹳足大王铜像诸
天佛殿公急下山见术
兵藏公劝勿入速逃公
迁入见李与赵藩坐公
政礼李怒曰佛教何用
有何益公曰圣人设教
总以济世利民语其初
基为善去恶涤古政教
孟行政以办民教以化
佛教教人治心心为万
物之本李得其正万物
得以宁而天下太平李
色窘以手指佛像。
宣化曰
化凶为吉矣。

**152**

## Changing misfortune to auspiciousness
## with a few words

The Provincial Commander stationed his troops at Hsi Tan
Monastery. They proceeded to destroy the copper image of the Great
King on Gold Peak of Chicken Foot Mountain, as well as the
Buddhahall and other shrines. The Master urgently descended the
mountain, and guards who recognized him urged him to go no further,
but to quickly flee while he could. The Master entered anyway, and
saw Commander Li with Chao Fan and greeted them. Li wrathfully
asked, "What good is Buddhism? What benefit does it give?" The
Master calmly answered, "The Sage established the Teachings to save
the world and benefit the people by its primary principle of exhorting
them to do good and turn away from evil. From ancient times, the
government and the teachings have complemented each other in
function, the former to set in order the masses, and the latter to
transform them. Buddhism teaches people how to effectively govern
their minds, which is the basis of the ten thousand things. If the
foundation is properly ordered, the ten thousand things will be at ease,
and there will be peace under heaven." At this, Li's fierce anger
ebbed, as he held out a hand to the Buddha image.

It was said:

He changed misfortune to auspiciousness.

片言改惡向善

又曰要這泥塑木雕作
麼空費錢財公曰佛言
法相相以表法不以相
表於法不張令人起敬
畏之心耳人若無敬
畏惡念作若不惡。
禍亂以成尼山塑聖丁
蘭刻木中圖祠宇各圖
銅像無非令人心有所
敬起其敬心功敬不可
思議語其極則若見諸
相非相即見如來李現
悅客呼具茶点請坐談。
宣化曰
改惡向善矣

## 153

## Changing evil to good with a few more words

The Commander further asked, "What use are those statues made of clay and wood? Isn't it a waste of money?" The Master answered, "The Buddha said that the marks of Dharma are just its symbols, the latter being used to represent the Dharma. Without representation through marks, the Dharma would not develop. Moreover, its expression brings about an attitude of reverence and awe, without which there are no evil deeds from which people would refrain, and no good deeds which they would perform. Calamity and chaos would result. Consider how they carved the statues of the sage Confucius upon Ni Ch'iu Mountain and how Ting Lan sculpted a wooden image of his deceased parents[21]. These images in the ancestral halls of China, as well as the copper ones from various other countries, serve as a place of reliance for the heart of man. They can foster an attitude of reverence, the effect of which is inconceivable. But in an ultimate sense, if one sees that all marks are no marks, one sees the Tathagata." Li was pleased and invited the Master to sit and chat, and called for tea and cakes.

It was said:

He changed evil into good.

---

[21.] Ting Lan was a famous filial son who lived in the Han Dynasty. His parents died when he was still too young to serve them. Upon growing up, Ting Lan fashioned wooden images of his parents and paid his respects to them through their statues. Morning and night he lit incense and bowed before the statues, as if they were his live parents. However, his wife got tired of this affair and one day, in jest, stuck a needle into the finger of one of the wooden statues. The wooden statue bled. When Ting Lan returned home, he saw to his dismay that the wooden statues were weeping tears. Upon questioning his wife, he found out the reason. Then he divorced his wife.

聆教府立教禮

李曰美如和尚不良
何公曰僧有聖有凡不
能見一二不肖而棄。
豈因一二不肖秀才。
罵孔子即先生統兵。
雖軍紀嚴明其一二。
皆如先生之聰明正
直乎海不棄魚蝦所
以為大者也。
宣化僧曰
佛法性海無不容僧
弘聖化用彌窮協統
聆教府然立教神立
正又鞠躬。

# 154

## Moving the commander, who, upon hearing the teachings, stood in awe and bowed

Li inquired, "But why are there monks who are not good?"

"There are both sagely and common members of the Sangha," the Master answered. "One cannot see one or two who are worthless and then discredit the rest because of them. One cannot revile Confucius because there are one or two despicable scholars. You, sir, are a commander of soldiers, and although your military discipline is strict, your troops are individuals. Do you expect that all of them be as intelligent and forthright as you? The ocean does not reject a single fish or shrimp, and therein lies its greatness."

The gatha says:

> In the sea-like nature of the Buddhadharma
>     nothing is excluded.
> The Sangha propagates the Sagely teaching,
>     its workings infinite.
> As the Provincial Commander heard the doctrines,
>     he stood in reverence and awe.
> He respectfully bowed, stood up erect,
>     then bowed again.

夜受教日自新
苗公晚齋東熠談由
因果分明說到業個
交織由業采因緣說
到世界眾生相續相
緣言愈暢而理愈深。
李時以溫語接公時
以容貌礼公平乃喟
然太息曰佛法廣大
多此吾已敕僧毀寺
業重奈何。
宣化偈曰
公云凤氣時使然極力
保護功大烏李公大悅
唯依敕同僧蔬食上殿參

**155**

## Having received the teaching in the evening, the commander renewed himself the next day

Li begged the Master to stay for a vegetarian meal. A candle was lit and the discussion turned to such topics as the clear discernment of cause and effect, the intricate weave of the net of karma, karmic retribution, causes and conditions, and the continuity of the world and living beings. The conversation was pleasant and the principles profound. Li's words revealed his gentle courtesy toward the Master, and his manner reflected great reverence for him. Suddenly, Li sighed deeply and said, "The Buddhadharma is extensive indeed, but I have killed Sangha members and ruined monasteries – my karma surely is heavy. What can I do about it?"

The gatha says:

> The Master said it was due to the influence
>     of these present times,
> But if he ardently protected the Dharma,
>     his merit would be great.
> Commander Li was very happy,
>     relying on the Teachings.
> Together with the monks, eating pure food,
>     he joined them in the ceremonies.

懺悔皈依三寶

迨八月四日山中忽
大現金光自山頂及
蓁草木皆變金黃色。
傳山中有佛銀金三
光佛光時有金銀僅
數現李孟威動執弟
子言神皈依三寶請
公為雞山總住持率
兵下山去山後若那
至德然化宣諭轉其
念於頃刻手搶公其可當
宣化偈曰
威武不屈大丈夫敢然往
見志何如填求怕死貪生
草逸之天々在歧途

**156**

## Helping the commander repent and take refuge with the Triple Jewel

Later, on the fourth day of the eighth lunar month, people observed a brilliant ray of golden light, which extended from the summit to the foot of the mountain. The flowers, grasses, and trees all turned a golden-yellow hue. It is said that on the mountain there are to be seen three types of light: Buddha Light, Silver Light, and Golden Light. Although the Buddha Light is occasionally seen, the Silver and Golden Lights rarely appear. Li was greatly moved by this occurrence, and seeking to become a disciple of the Master, took refuge with the Triple Jewel. He requested the Master to assume the general Abbotship of Chi Tsu (Chicken Foot) Mountain, and led his troops down the mountain. If it were not for the Master's eminent virtue in this quiet transformation, how could he have changed the man's thoughts in such a short period of time? Who else but the Master would have been capable of this?

The gatha says:

> Martial sternness could not intimidate
>     the great hero.
> The Master boldly went to see him;
>     this was his resolve.
> Laughable are living beings who are
>     greedy to live and afraid to die,
> And who run amok on treacherous paths.

至滬成立佛教總會

滬佛會秋革制。略典
諸方撤韜電公徃晤。
寄禪治開晤帝太虗。
仁山諦閑諸師協商
委善設佛教總會於
靜安寺南京晤孫中
山商政訂會章畢復
興寄禪至北京表
世凱寄公病於法源
寺生脫公扶柩玉滬
閑佛教總會成立會
宣化偈曰
佛教總會設靜安默藏
文公布遠印泉李公函介
銘蔡松坡等外護賢

**157**

## Going to Shanghai and establishing the Buddhist Association

Because of a new regime, the Buddhist organizations in Shanghai met with conflict on all sides, and telegraphed the Master, asking him to come. He met and discussed the situation with Dharma Masters Chi Ch'an, Chih K'ai, P'u Ch'ang, T'ai Hsü, Jen Shan, and Ti Hsien. It was agreed and arranged that a Buddhist Association would be established with headquarters at Ching An (Quiet Peace) Monastery. In Nanking, the Master conferred with Dr. Sun Yat-sen, and discussed the revising of the Association's by-laws. Later, he went to Peking with Dharma Master Chi Ch'an and met with Yüan Shih-kai. Dharma Master Chi Ch'an became ill at Fa Yüan (Dharma Source) Monastery, and left the world while sitting up. The Master returned to Shanghai with the coffin, and later convened the opening ceremonies for the Buddhist Association.

The gatha says:

>The Chinese Buddhist Association
>>was established at Ching An.
>To Yunnan and Kueichow Provinces
>>he brought the news in Tibetan.
>Li Yin Ch'uan gave the Master
>>letters of introduction.
>Telling General Ts'ai Sung P'o
>>and others to protect the holy.

## 八哥鳥念彌陀

壬子七十三歲公回
滇後即開辦佛教分
會在文昌宮開成立
大會請了座師說分
會於貴州藏剌嘛來
者甚眾擬舉辦佛教
學校佛道醫院等。
惡善事業有人送一
八哥鳥放生能言初食間
飯依學念佛吃素一日被
鷹提去　宣化偈曰
飛空空中仍念佛盡此
報身生極樂胡為離物
之靈者人不及鳥惡姿
婆。

**158**

## Liberating a mynah that recited Amitabha

In 1912, when the Master was seventy-three years old, after returning
to Yunnan Province, he began to set up branches of the Buddhist
Association. At Wen Chang Hall, he convened a large meeting, at
which he asked Dharma Master Liao Ch'en (Ending the Dust) to
establish a branch in Kueichow Province. A large number of Tibetan
Lamas took part, and it was decided to organize Buddhist schools,
groups for spreading the Dharma, and hospitals, among other means
of performing philanthropic works. Someone donated a mynah bird,
which was to be set free. The bird could talk, and at first ate flesh; but
after receiving the Refuges, it learned to recite the Buddha's name,
and became a vegetarian. One day, it was seized and carried off by an
eagle.

The gatha says:

> Carried off, flying through the air,
>     it still recited the Buddha's name.
> At the end of this retribution body,
>     it was born in Ultimate Bliss.
> If people are the magic essence
>     of the ten thousand things,
> Then how can we measure up to this bird
>     if we linger on in the Saha World?

## 寃魂索命報仇

癸丑七十四歲為會赴入京。見鍾希齡。內向據琤往可。澄慕維護佛教甲寅辛五歲回雞山班工程進歲十三大寺乙卯七十六歲舂歲期。畢有鄧川鼎丁孝廉女年十八一日忽不省人事表醒。寶男聲大馬其父回汝侍勢詆我為匪至喪我命我即董占亂海遠汜浮否今闓王准報八年之仇語畢持刀逐丁。宣化偶曰因果不可逃造業必受報今日鬼索命往時心喪拍。

**159**

## An avenging spirit demands a life in repayment

The Master was seventy-four in 1913, and had gone to the capital on important Buddhist Assocation affairs. He spoke with Prime Minister Hsiung Hsi Ling and Minister of the Interior Jen K'e Ch'eng, whose efforts helped to protect Buddhism. In 1914, the Master, then seventy-five, returned to Chicken Foot Mountain, where he oversaw the repair of monasteries and temples. Traveling through Tibet, he visited thirteen great monasteries. The Master was seventy-six in 1915. After the transmission of the precepts in the spring, the eighteen-year-old daughter of an imperial scholar named Ting, a native of Teng Ch'üan county, suddenly lapsed into a coma. Upon waking, she spoke with a male-sounding voice, and angrily accused her father, saying, "You presumed upon your position to falsely accuse me of being a thief and are therefore responsible for my death. I am Tung Chan Piao; do you remember? King Yama has allowed me to avenge this eight-year grudge!" With that, she grabbed a knife and chased after Ting.

The gatha says:

Cause and effect cannot be escaped.
Making karma, you must receive the retribution.
If today a ghost demands your life,
It is because of your murderous mind in the past.

辭寬說戒拜師

鬼曰必來秉女則變形態家
攘攘鄉里縣觀苦之時雞
山派眾琴秉値二僧往鄧
川公脫至丁家群觀鬼凶
狀僧曰勸你不要這樣令
地方不安鬼曰你出家人
不要多事僧曰本與我無干
我師父常由寬家宜辭不
宜辭愈德愈深何時淳了鬼
思有頃曰你師是誰僧曰祝
聖寺虛雲和尚鬼曰五百飯
依受戒。
宣化偈曰　親送至雞山。
雲公說戒壇虛此辭寬
結鄧川結會懺。

# 160

## Freeing a ghost, explaining the precepts, and bowing in repentance

Each day, as the disgruntled ghost came, the girl's manner and behavior would drastically and abruptly change. Not only was her family disturbed, but the neighbors were affected as well. At that time, the two monks Su Ch'in and Su Chih were sent by Chi Tsu Mountain to Teng Ch'üan County on monastery business. As they passed Ting's house, they noticed a crowd of people observing the malign appearance. One of the monks said to her, "I urge you to curtail this disturbance of the peace."

The ghost said, "Why don't you monks mind your own business?"

The monk answered, "This may not be my concern, but my teacher often says that enmity should be ended, not perpetuated, because the longer it is continued, the deeper it becomes. When will it end?"

The ghost reflected a moment, and then asked, "Who is your teacher?"

"The Venerable Abbot Hsü Yün of Chu Sheng (Celebration of Sageliness) Monastery."

The ghost said, "I wish to take refuge with him and receive the precepts."

The gatha says:

> They escorted the ghost back to Chi Tsu Mountain,
> Where the Venerable Yün explained
> the Precept Platform.
> From this, the bonds of enmity were sundered.
> In Teng Chüan County,
> repentance ceremonies were held.

横逆相加因緣錢

丙辰七十七歲高萬邦冰
送玉佛存供觀音亭已畢
年公欲請回豆。闻義族多
信佛者為往章達之帶寓
等地觀風。到緬請經附船
抵新街被檢驗誣為革命
完因之不唯動早六時至
晚八時有飯依弟子洪戚
祥明五千元一人保釋六
僧盡手即放出至戚祥簡
店當度年助料理蓮玉
佛事。
宣化偈曰　誣為革命
党捕房因六僧圇圄
共患難佛國同化生。

# 161

## Being bound and incarcerated
## for no good reason

It was 1916, and the Master was seventy-seven. Several years had passed since he had intended to bring back the jade Buddha donated by Upasaka Kao Wan Pang, which was being stored at the Kuan Yin Pavilion in Penang, Malaysia. Moreover, the Master had heard that there were many natives in that area who believed in the Buddha, so again he set out for the countries of the South Seas to visit various places there. In Burma, he lectured a Sutra. Later, arriving by ship in Singapore, the Master was questioned and falsely accused of being a revolutionary. He was detained from 6 a.m. to 8 p.m., when finally a disciple, Hung Sheng Hsiang, who had previously taken refuge with the Master, arrived and paid the bail of five thousand dollars each for the party of six monks. The seal was affixed, and they went to Sheng Hsiang's place of business, where he entreated the Master to stay until after the New Year. Materials for the transportation of the jade Buddha back to China were donated.

The gatha says:

> Falsely accused of being revolutionaries,
> The six Sanghans were incarcerated.
> Enduring hardships together in prison,
> They'll be born by transformation in Buddhalands.

舉巨石服群眾

丁巳七十八歲春由
觀音亭起運玉佛催
八工人舁之送至鵝
山行教十日山嶺崎
嶇人跡未到屬一日
行至野人山工人疑
玉佛內有金寶置佛
於地言力不勝起價。
善言不聽似有不利
者。瞥見巨石教百斤
重公指謂佛与石孰重。
曰三倍之公力舉石工者
畏服曰老和尚活佛也遂
佛至山厚賞之去
宣化曰 護法默助也。

# 162

## Moving a boulder and winning workmen's respect

The Master's seventy-eighth year was 1917. In the spring, eight workers were hired to transport the jade Buddha from Kuan Yin Pavilion to Chicken Foot Mountain in China, a journey of quite a few days over treacherous mountain paths and places where no people had previously gone. One day while passing through Yeh Jen (Wild Men) Mountain, the workers got the idea that there were gold and gems inside the Buddha, which they consequently refused to carry further, saying that they had no strength to do so. They raised their fee and would not listen to reason, as if someone were taking advantage of them. The Master noticed a boulder of several hundred pounds to which he pointed and said, "Is this rock not heavier than the Buddha?" The workers agreed that it was two or three times heavier. The Master then raised the boulder over his head, and the workers were completely awed. They said, "This Venerable Master is a living Buddha!" They carried the Buddha image through the mountains and were generously rewarded by the Master upon arrival at their destination.

It was said:

The Dharma Protectors silently lent their aid.

水陸感應祥瑞

戊午年七十九歲唐繼
堯督軍禮請赴昆明作
佛事公偕徒俗圓繼途
遇匪說服至滇見唐云
敬行三事〈一〉作一場大
佛事求佛加被消災免
難超荐亡靈〈二〉建大齋
林宏揚佛法〈三〉加一完
善大學教育青年公曰
我六定三事柴屠大教
賑濟間始煙皆卍未八十歲
彩尊目七七圓滿送聖靈
中獻憧幡寶蓋
宣佈曰 感應雖思

# 163

## Performing a "Water and Land" ceremony, which brought auspicious omens

In 1918, when the Master was seventy-nine, the Military Governor T'ang Chi Yao respectfully invited him to come to Kunming to perform Buddhist ceremonies. The Master set out with a disciple named Hsiu Yüan (Perfect Cultivation), but en route they encountered bandits whom the Master convinced to desist. Arriving in Kunming, he met with T'ang, who stated his three intentions, as follows: 1) to convene a large Buddhist assembly to seek the support of the Buddhas in eradicating disasters and misfortune, and in crossing over the spirits of the dead; 2) to establish a large monastery in order to propagate the Buddhadharma; and 3) to set up a college for the education of the young. The Master told him, "I also have three suggestions: 1) Prohibit the slaughter of animals for meat; 2) proclaim a general amnesty; and 3) send relief for those in distress." It was done, and in 1919, when the Master turned eighty, the Dharma assembly began. The flames of the candles took on the shape of lotus blossoms, and their rainbows of colors dazzled the eye. At the completion of forty-nine days, during the Sages Ceremony of Sending Off, jeweled canopies appeared in the sky, along with banners and flags.

It was said:

An inconceivable response!

双鵝念佛往生

庚申八十一歲唐督請公
住華亭寺唐卦港張拙
仙以雌雄二鵝送雲樓寺
放生請說皈依佈靜聽
說戒畢你善狀隨人上殿
誦經繞佛於是三年雌鵝
於佛前右繞三匝屹立蛻
去不久雄者亦然毛形不
萎盛以木盒葬之一塚。

宣化偈曰
一切眾生有佛性百
千三昧證菩提萬物
原來本一體三界會
私住自通。

**164**

## Two Geese, mindful of the Buddha, go off to rebirth

The Master was eighty-one in 1920, and Governor T'ang invited him to stay in Hua T'ing (Flower Pavilion) Monastery. Later, T'ang went to Hong Kong. One day Chang Ch'ou Hsien brought a pair of geese, one male and one female, to be set free at Yün Ch'i (Cloud Abode) Monastery. He requested the Master speak the refuges for them. The geese lowered their heads and quietly listened, and after the precepts were explained, they appeared happy. For the subsequent three years, they followed along with the assembly during the ceremonies, Sutra recitation, and circumambulating of the Buddha. Then one day, the female goose walked around the Buddhas to the right three times, stood up straight and left her body. It was not long after that the male followed along. At death, their feathers did not wilt, but remained fresh. The geese were placed in small wooden boxes, and buried.

The gatha says:

Every single living being
    has the Buddha nature.
In hundreds of thousands of different samadhis
    they are certified to enlightenment.
The source of the ten thousand things
    is but a single substance.
To be devoid of self in the three phases of time
    is to gain complete self-mastery.

救溺女度二姓

辛酉八十二歲顧吧珍督
滇滂旱疫疾喉病頻一
切暫緩進行一日公赴
滇回憩樹下拾一包裹。
開視金玉釧珠錄等滇
儘人取已晚暫回至海
有女投海拯救之詢乃
朱姓嫁孫師長以受氣
故攜欵逃而然公化雙
方家皈依受戒
宣化偈曰 失金欵自
救恰遇活菩薩拯救雖
苦海孫朱共獻花。

# 165

## Saving a drowning girl and rescuing two families

In 1921, the Master's eighty-second year, Ku P'in Chen was the governor of Yunnan Province. During that year a flood, a drought, and a diphtheria epidemic followed in close succession, and all progress was slowed considerably. One day, when the Master was resting under a tree on his way back from the city, he found and opened a package. It contained gold and jade bracelets, a watch as well as eight thousand Yunnan dollars, and over ten thousand dollars in French francs among other things. Closing the package, he waited for the owner to come and claim it. But since it was late, he decided to return the next day. Upon reaching the lake, the Master saved a girl who had cast herself into the water. The girl later revealed that her name was Chu, and that she had married an army commander named Sun. Because she had been mistreated, she had fled with her valuables and belongings. The Master converted the families of both the husband and wife, transmitting to them both the Refuges and Precepts.

The gatha says:

> Having lost her money,
>     she wanted to commit suicide,
> But luckily encountered a live Bodhisattva
> Who pulled her out of the sea of suffering.
> Then Sun and Chu together offered flowers.

拾遺金賑災黎

壬戌八十三歲重修華亭
寺乃阿育次子見碧風一
群而名碧雞山掘土得碑
有雲樓二字又於後山林
中拾一包袱內有金銀幣
等二十餘萬元賑議歌
歸常住公則主張獻與
政府賑濟鰥寡孤獨災
難困者百姓報稱善。
宣化偈曰
路不拾遺古聖時。
富義取斯人知飢饉
布施航濟報捨己涘
善大德師

# 166

## Contributing gold to aid those stricken by disaster

The remodeling of Hua T'ing (Floral Pavilion) Monastery began in 1922, the Master's eighty-third year. In ancient times, the second son of King Ashoka had seen a flock of jade phoenixes there, which is why the mountain was named Jade Bird Mountain. During the process of excavating for the reconstruction, an ancient stone tablet was found, upon which were carved the words "Yün Ch'i" (Cloud Abode). Also, in the mountain forest behind the monastery, a parcel of more than 200,000 dollars in gold and silver was found. The community was intending to donate it to the Eternally Dwelling, but the Master proposed giving it to the government instead in order to aid widowers, the destitute, orphans and the solitary. That way the disasters and suffering of the masses would be relieved. Everyone agreed.

The gatha says:

> What was left behind was not picked up
>      in the time of the ancient sages.
> The Master knew propriety
>      and did not keep the treasure.
> He turned it over to the famine's victims
>      to relieve the suffering masses.
> Forgetting himself and pursuing the good,
>      he was a greatly virtuous Master!

暮春祈雪消喉疾

滇連年災異迭乘喉病
大作數月不雨死亡軍
官民無數群思唐公政
德議決滇請唐公住督
滇唐洎寺請公設壇祈
雨采大雨三日而喉疾
未除須雪治方可時在
暮春唐仍請公祈雪治
喉設壇日采大雪盈尺。
報信佛法難思

宣化偈曰
暮春瑞雪紛紛飄消除
喉疫救同胞唐公善政
天心轉長老慈願佛
力略。

# 167

## Praying for snow near the end of spring to end diphtheria

Yunnan Province had seen serious disasters for several years in a row. The diphtheria epidemic continued, and there had been no rain for several months. Members of the military, public officials, and citizens perished in large numbers. Remembering the excellent administration of ex-governor T'ang, the community met and invited him to return and resume his former duties. T'ang came to the monastery and requested the Master to set up an altar to pray for rain, and as a result, it poured for three days. The diphtheria epidemic continued, however, because only a snowfall could bring it to an end. Spring was drawing to a close, and Governor T'ang requested that the Master pray for snow to end the disease. An altar was set up, and when a large snowfall ensued, all the people believed in the inconceivability of the Buddhadharma.

The gatha says:

> Towards the end of spring, auspicious snow
> floated everywhere.
> It totally stopped the diphtheria
> and saved our countrymen.
> The honorable T'ang was good at governing,
> influencing heaven to change its mind.
> The Buddha's strength lends its aid to
> the Elder Master's compassionate vows.

荒年割稻與民食

癸亥八十四歲時現李氏
化蓮道明蟻塔具行自
化生西等黑蹖甲子八十
歲修諸經塔寺乙丑八十六歲
傳戒誦經起長七丙寅八十
七歲近年滇境多兵劫民
畏稻熟而不敢收公向官
請以僧領收勿阻故千人
聚食始飯健粥辣水等其
甚著民德之

宣化偈曰
始則同食飯健而飲粥
粥修至糜和水僧佑
共英富

**168**

## Reaping rice during a barren year and feeding the people

In 1923, the Master was eighty-four. At that time, several strange events were witnessed: a transformational lotus appeared upon the cremation of Mrs. Li; a pagoda was made by ants for Bhikshu Tao Ming; and Bhikshu Chü Hsing transformed himself and attained birth in the West. Next year, 1924, the Master was eighty-five, and spent time rebuilding various shrines and temples. In 1925, when the Master was eighty-six, he transmitted the precepts, explained sutras, and held long meditation sessions. The Master was eighty-seven in the year 1926. In the ensuing few years, large numbers of soldiers plundered Yunnan Province, frightening the people. The rice was ripe, but they did not dare harvest it. The Master, therefore, asked the Army commander not to allow his troops to obstruct the harvest, which was subsequently carried out by the monks. Because of the lack of food, one thousand peasants gathered at the monastery to take their meals. At first, rice was eaten, then gruel, then chaff, and finally just water was all that remained. The people appreciated the fact that the monks underwent the same hardships of life along with them.

The gatha says:

> At first they all ate rice alike,
>     and then drank thin rice gruel.
> Finally they took just chaff and water,
>     the monks and the peasants eating together.

菜梅間蓮兆瑞

公往持靈楊寺備材鳩工。
親捧勞役建等僧坊完
成後每年皆傳僧戒法講
經教坐禪香兩寅戒期
中殿前老枯梅樹間白
蓮花數十朵前後菜園
中青菜皆開青蓮花華
中皆有化佛儼然如我
今盧舍那方坐蓮華台。
周匝千華上復現千釋
迦。　　宣化偈曰
枯梅間蓮華。主林神
助菩諸佛來加護千
葉千釋迦。

# 169

## Witnessing the auspicious omen of greens and plum trees blooming with lotuses

As the Abbot of Yün Ch'i (Cloud Abode) Monastery, the Master prepared construction materials, assembled workmen, and himself joined in the painstaking labor of reconstruction. A new monastery was built. Upon its completion, the precepts were transmitted every year, the teachings of the sutras were explained, and there was practice of dhyana meditation. During the precept ceremony of 1926, the old and withered plum trees in front of the main hall blossomed with a large number of white lotus flowers. Throughout the vegetable garden, the greens bloomed into green lotuses. In each of the flowers was a majestic transformational Buddha, re-enacting the following Sutra passage:

> Now I, the Buddha Nishyanda
> sit here atop the lotus dais.
> All around, upon a thousand flowers,
> appear a thousand Shakyan Lords.

The gatha says:

> The withered plum trees bloomed with lotuses
> Appearing through the aid of the forest-ruling spirits.
> Buddhas came to protect the location.
> There were thousands of Shakyamunis upon
> thousands of lotus petals!

赴香港搏鼓山

丁卯八十八歲建幽冥
鐘樓等工程戊辰八十九
歲為募佛像欵同王九
齡居士至香港時陳真
如主粵政派員接公至
廣州進白雲山陳擬留
公住持南華寺重振
曹溪道場公卻之回閩
至鼓山誦經畢赴育
王捨舍利朝普陀
宣化偶回　為募善
緣涉山川晝令同倫種
福田育緣即栽無漏果。
當面錯過萬劫難。

# 170

## Going to Hong Kong and Ku[22] Mountain

The bell tower for the dead and other construction projects were completed in 1927, the Master's eighty-eighth year. The following year, in order to raise money for the making of Buddha images, the Master went to Hong Kong accompanied by Upasaka Wang Chiu Ling. At that time, Ch'en Chen Ju, head of the Kuangtung Provincial Government, sent his representative to escort the Master to Canton. They passed by Pai Yün (White Cloud) Mountain, and later, Ch'en urged the Master to stay and assume Abbotship of Nan Hua Monastery[23], to restore the famous Bodhimanda at Ts'ao Hsi (Creek). The Master declined, and returned to Drum Mountain in Fukien Province where he lectured a sutra. When it was completed, he bowed to the Buddha's sharira at King Ashoka Temple and made a pilgrimage to P'u T'ou (Potala) Mountain.

The gatha says:

> In order to set up wholesome conditions
>> he crossed the mountains and rivers,
> Universally causing everyone
>> to sow the field of blessings.
> By nurturing such affinities,
>> beings can reap the fruit of no outflows.
> If we miss this opportunity when it presents itself,
>> it   will be difficult to encounter in ten thousand kalpas.

---

22. "Drum"
23. The monastery of the Venerable Master Hui Neng, the Sixth Patriarch in China.

就任湧泉寺住持

己巳九十歲正月在滬起
程回鼓山禮祖塔墓有間
主席東海軍部長楊幼京
(樹莊)與前住主席方丈虛雲
率官紳僧俗居士護法
等函公住持鼓山丈席。
公以鼓山乃薙染初地俛
悵祖德義不容辭責難。
推諉逐允就住整理寺風。
宣化偈曰

湧泉古剎唐代興。高
僧龍象度群萌雲公
飛錫駐石鼓数正頓宗
風敎化行。

# 171

## Becoming abbot of Yung Ch'üan[24] Monastery

The Master was ninety years old in 1929. During the first month of that year, he left Shanghai for Ku (Drum) Mountain, where he bowed to the stupas of the Patriarchs. Yang Yu Ching (Shu Chuang), the Chief Executive of Fukien Province and Secretary of the Navy, and Fang Sheng T'ao, the former Chief Executive, headed a group of public officials, scholars, monks, laymen, and other protectors of the Dharma to urge the Master to become Chief Abbot of Drum Mountain. This was where the Master first shaved his head and donned the monk's robes. As he recalled with strong sentiment his virtuous predecessors, he could not neglect his duty or retire from his responsibility. He accepted their request and set about restoring the monastery to its former glory.

The gatha says:

> The ancient shrine of Bubbling Spring
> > flourished during the T'ang.
> There High Sanghans – dragons and elephants –
> > crossed over the multitudes.
> The tin staff of Master Yün
> > was planted in a drum of stone,
> As he restored the School's renown,
> > through his teaching and cultivation.

---

24. "Bubbling Spring"

丹墀及鐵樹開花

庚午九十一歲所荷一切敕
緒春戒期請文質和尚
為羯磨諸覺綱經時方
丈室前丹墀中兩株鐵
樹威開花朵據傳此樹
乃閩王與聖前祖師名
手植一株甚雄生長千
年始開華一次以彰其瑞。
公有偈誌優曇奸羅非
凡品云之。
宣化偈曰　菩薩演法
眾護持故光現瑞正及
時空中傳報龍天賀鐵
樹開華世稀奇。

# 172

## Witnessing a pair of cycad trees
## blooming in the courtyard

At ninety-one years of age in 1930, the Master continued to transmit the precepts in the spring as he had done every year. He requested the Venerable Master Wen Chih to be the Karmadana, While he was lecturing the *Brahmajala (Brahma Net) Sutra*, two feathery palm trees in the courtyard in front of the Abbot's quarters bloomed with many lush blossoms. Tradition states that both the king of the state of Min and Patriarch Sheng Chien (Sagely Arrow) had each planted one of the trees. Their growth had been very slow, for it normally takes that kind of tree one thousand years to bloom. Because of the auspiciousness of the event, the Master wrote a verse, one line of which says:

Udumbara flowers are not at all a common sight.

The gatha says:

The Bodhisattva proclaims the Dharma;
    the masses protect and maintain it.
An auspicious appearance emitting light –
    the time for it was ripe.
The news was communicated in the sky;
    the dragons and gods praised it.
The cycad trees bloomed with flowers
    – strange and rare indeed!

重戒律開办学院

辛未九十一歲公為宗門
泰斗提倡向上一法教外
別傳直指人心見性成佛。
不立文字以心印心主法。
復以末法僧伽不重戒律
故創办戒律學院作育
佛教新青年紹隆正法。
請慈舟律師為主講法。
師學僧六七十人眾。
宣化偈曰
提倡本义造僧材十方
學者歸去來主講律佛
委恶老大闡尸羅金
剛戒。

**173**

## Establishing an academy for intensive Vinaya

The Master was ninety-two in 1931, and was esteemed as the leader of the Ch'an school of Buddhism. He taught that the method of attaining the One lay in the "special transmission outside the teaching; direct pointing to the heart; seeing the nature and becoming a Buddha; a method which is not dependent on language, but which is the mind-to-mind transmission." Moreover, because the Sangha in these Dharma-ending times did not lay emphasis on the moral code, the Master organized a Vinaya Academy to educate young Buddhists in accord with the Proper Dharma. Vinaya Master Tz'u Chou (Compassionate Boat) was invited to be the senior lecturer. Some sixty to seventy monks enrolled.

The gatha says:

> He promoted the Pratimoksha
> and developed Sangha talent,
> And students from the ten directions
> returning home, arrived.
> The Venerable Tz'u was chosen as
> chief-lecturing Vinaya Master.
> He clearly explained the Shila Code,
> that is, the Vajra Precepts.

老龍神受寶戒

壬申九十三歲春戒期中，有
一老叟鬚髮雪白。戒期中看
清奇。直入丈室跪余前言
來求戒。問其姓氏。云閩南
台橋人。姓楊。時有計戒妙
宗。亦南台人。詢之不識此
老者菩薩戒畢。即失蹤。
妙宗回南台進龍王廟。
神像儼然受戒老者。

宣化偈曰

龍王求戒化老翁菩薩
戒畢影無蹤妙師經
過龍神側戒牒端然
在手中。

# 174

## Transmitting the jeweled precepts
## to an old dragon spirit

During the Spring Precept Transmission period of 1932, when the
Master was in his ninety-third year, an old man with snow-white hair
and beard and an unusual manner arrived and went directly to the
Abbot's quarters. Kneeling before the Master, he said he had come to
seek the precepts. When asked his name, he replied that he was called
Yang, and was a native of Nan T'ai Chiao in Fukien Province. At that
time, there happened to be a newly precepted monk from Nan T'ai
named Miao Tsung in residence. When asked, the latter said he did
not know the old man, who disappeared after the transmission of the
Bodhisattva Precepts. Dharma Master Miao Tsung returned to Nan
T'ai, and upon entering the Lung Wang (Dragon King) Temple, was
startled to discover that the image of the majestic spirit showed he
was none other than the old man who had just received the precepts!

The gatha says:

> The Dragon King, seeking the precepts,
> > turned into an old man.
> The Bodhisattva Precepts once transmitted,
> > he was gone without a trace.
> But when Dharma Master Miao himself
> > passed by the Dragon Spirit,
> The latter held right in his hand
> > a precept certificate!

维乱世犹海军

癸酉九四岁。日本进入
山海闽民〈惊慌〉兵乱
纷纷到处全省寺院。
在闽举事
均此单惟鼓山公住持
故仍面海单十方海报。
云水僧人云集於鼓山
者数达千五六百之多。
斋粮困难处仍维持一
粥一饭水准。
宣化偈曰  佛教已任担
为来僧伽饥渴身受帐。
患难颠沛必於是世变
流离更宜栽。

**175**

## Despite the unrest, still receiving visitors by sea

In 1933, the Master was ninety-four. The Japanese Army occupied Shan Hai Kuan and caused great trepidation among the people. Soldiers were reckless and unruly. Unrest was widespread. In Fukien, the Nineteenth Army started an uprising. All the other temples and monasteries in the province stopped receiving visitors. However, because the Master was Abbot, Ku (Drum) Mountain continued to receive monks coming by sea. Wandering bhikshus from the ten directions gathered in large numbers at Drum Mountain. Supplying adequate food for all was difficult, since there might be as many as fifteen or sixteen hundred, and rationing permitted just one bowl of gruel and one bowl of rice per day per person.

The gatha says:

> Personally bearing the Buddha's teaching,
>    he carried it on into the future,
> While bodies of the Sangha members
>    were subject to hunger and thirst.
> Times of trouble and difficulty
>    are a certainty,
> So wandering through this changing world
>    is the best place to cultivate.

三夢六祖來名

甲戌九十五歲。春戒邀應慈法師。講梵網經二月一夕作趺坐時君夢非夢。見六祖大師至曰時至矣。汝富回去翌日語弟子覬。本嚮之四月間一夕又三夢六祖催去公覽甚異。未武有粵主席李漢魂。派吳鍾石等持書請之。宣化偈曰

六祖三夢催速回。百官萬民迎法軀寶林道場重光日。苦行老僧挑土時。

# 176

## Seeing the Sixth Patriarch arrive three times to summon him

In 1934, the Master, now ninety-five, invited Dharma Master Ying Tz'u to explain the *Brahmajala (Brahma Net) Sutra* during the spring Precept period. One night, in the second lunar month, while sitting cross-legged in meditation, as if in a dream and yet not at all in a dream, the Master saw the Sixth Patriarch arrive and tell him, "The time has come for you to return." The following day, the Master told his disciple Kuan Pen about this vision. The latter consoled him. One evening, in the fourth lunar month, he again on three occasions saw the Sixth Patriarch who urged him to go. The Master thought this event quite strange. Shortly thereafter, General Li Han Yün of Canton sent Wu Chung Shih and others with an invitation for the Master, which the Master accepted.

The gatha says:

> Appearing thrice, the Venerable Sixth Patriarch
> urged him to quickly go back.
> A hundred officials and ten thousand citizens
> welcomed the embodied Dharma.
> The bodhimanda at Jeweled Grove
> again shone like the sun,
> Because it was time for the old ascetic monk
> to carry earth once more.

人受戒虎皈依

冬諸護法堅請受戒額
垣破屋不能住衆加搭
蔡逢竹屋住客粵韶官
紳眷屬來數百人節兵
保術皈依者甚眾冬月
十七日入夜說菩薩戒時
虎來皈依大眾譁然公
為說皈戒三叩首馴然
曰虎誠皈依佛正忘爰兩
樣公與畜忘同一光明藏
宣化偈曰
獸王禮法王皈依護戒
壇年年來朝拜月
月持戒香

**177**

## Giving precepts to the people and letting a tiger take refuge

During the winter, the Dharma protectors persistently requested that the Master transmit the precepts; but the walls of the buildings had collapsed, and the dwellings were all but destroyed. They were uninhabitable, so makeshift structures of thatched palm and bamboo were put up for the guests to stay in. The gentry of Canton and Shao Chou arrived with their households, several hundred people in all, bringing soldiers for protection. A large number of people took refuge. On the seventeenth day of the eleventh lunar month, during the transmission of the Bodhisattva Precepts, night had fallen when suddenly a tiger arrived to take refuge. Everyone was aghast, but the Master transmitted the refuges and the precepts to him. The tiger bowed its head three times and was very tame. The Master said, "This tiger knows enough to take refuge with the Buddha. There are no two ways about it: the hearts of humans and the hearts of animals are equally endowed with a treasury of brilliance."

The gatha says:

> The King of Beasts bowed down
> to the King of Dharma,
> Taking refuge and protecting
> the Platform of the Precepts.
> Every year it came to prostrate
> itself in reverence,
> Month after month being perfumed with
> the fragrance of holding Precepts.

枯柏欣欣向榮

乙亥九十六歲春漢魂李
公調任東區典建二人
相助戒期後應港東華
三院請建水陸軍轉鼓
山請圓瑛法師任住持公
回南華修祖殿觀音堂。
寮房工程冬月寺後伏
虎亭北卓錫泉南有老
柏三株宋代植枯數百
年忽發新枝。
宣化偈曰　枯柏欣欣又
向榮生氣勃勃樂意濃。
筆者祝觀斯奇跡至
德感物靡不應。

# 178

## Joyously witnessing the revival of withered cypresses

The Master turned ninety-six in 1935. In the spring, General Li Han Yün was transferred to regions in the east, and so there was a lack of people to aid with the reconstruction projects. Following the precept period, the Master responded to an invitation by the Tung Hua Institution of Hong Kong to lead ceremonies to benefit those who had died on land or water. Upon its completion, he returned to Ku (Drum) Mountain and asked Dharma Master Yüan Ying to replace him as Abbot. Upon his return to Nan Hua Monastery, the Master renovated the Hall of the Patriarchs, built a new Kuan Yin Hall, and also some dormitories. Around the eleventh lunar month, three ancient cypress trees north of Fu Hu Pavilion and south of Cho Hsi Spring, which had been planted during the Sung Dynasty and had been dead for several hundred years, suddenly sprang to life.

The gatha says:

> The withered cypresses once again
>     gloriously revive,
> Flourishing in a burst of life,
>     exuding joyfulness.
> The author personally witnessed this
>     strange and wonderful event:
> The Master's ultimate virtue always
>     evoked responses from all living things.

白狐皈依守戒

丙子九十之歲春仍傳戒。
後有國府主席林公子
超居院長蔣公中正
等。來寺助脩各工程時
曹溪駐防十六團長林
國賡攜一白狐至欲放
生公為說皈依竟救之
山中不去如家犬守於
寺中後被車傷腿公為
說偈超度。
宣化偈曰　白狐皈依
更通靈蔣公驟至遠相
迎入文引公出見客彼
此握手笑盈盈。

# 179

## Letting a white fox take refuge and uphold the precepts

In the spring of 1936, the precepts were transmitted as usual. The Master was ninety-seven. Later, the Chief of State Lin Tzu Ch'ao, House Speaker Chü Cheng, and General Chiang Kai-shek, among others, came to the monastery and lent their aid to the renovation. At that time, the Sixteenth Route Army was garrisoned at Ts'ao Hsi, and its leader, Lin Kuo Keng, brought a white fox to the monastery to be set free. The Master explained to the fox the meaning of taking refuge, and it was released in the mountains. Refusing to leave, it remained in the monastery area like a pet dog. Later on it was injured by a cart, and the Master spoke a verse to cross over its spirit.

The gatha says:

> A white fox receiving the Triple Jewel
>     is truly magical,
> General Chiang arrived from afar,
>     and was heartily welcomed.
> The Master came out to greet
>     his guests,
> Shaking hands all around
>     and laughing heartily.

西藏活佛皈敬

丁丑九十八歲春戒畢公應
廣州居士林請赴穗講經。
時有西藏活佛榮增堪希
金剛上師與羅格更桑等。
十餘人慕道德而來皈
依佛山諸僧衆護法等。
請赴佛山為仁壽寺寶
塔開光回南華寺仍俗
造各院宇工程總料理。
宣化偈曰
廣闡法筵度含識大
南教義化泯衆西藏
活佛來敏敬東震比
丘第一枝。

# 180

## A Tibetan Lama respectfully requesting to take refuge

After the spring Precept Period of 1937, the Master, now ninety-eight, responded to an invitation by the Laypeople's Association of Canton to go there and explain a sutra. At that time, a Tibetan lama, Vajra Master Jung Tseng K'en Pu, arrived, accompanied by Lo Ke Keng Sang and ten others. Admiring the Master's virtue in the Way, they came to receive refuge. Later, members of the Sangha and protectors of the Dharma invited the Master to go to Fuo (Buddha) Mountain and conduct the Opening of the Light Ceremony at the Jeweled Pagoda at Jen Shou (Humane Age) Monastery. Returning to Nan Hua Monastery, the Master then continued to oversee the tasks of reconstruction there.

The gatha says:

> Setting forth a vast Dharma feast,
>     he crossed over many beings.
> Clearly expounding the teaching's meaning,
>     he transformed the ignorant masses.
> A Lama from Tibet
>     respectfully received the refuges.
> The land of China produced
>     an exceptionally first-rate bhikshu.

減食過午賑災

戊寅九十九歲仍傳戒講經。
赴港作大悲法會秋回南
華乙卯一百歲春戒期各
處兵難新戒益多十方
來聚公提倡每日禮佛二
小時以息災劫而超度
抗日戰事陣亡將士大
眾吃午減省晚食餘糧
獻與政府賑災報讚成。
宣化偈曰
慈善為懷賑災民須
達長者給孤貧老人
方外念赤子減食節
衣救群倫

# 181

## Eliminating the evening meal
## to relieve disaster victims

The Master was ninety-nine in 1938, and continued his annual transmission of the Precepts and lecturing of Sutras. In Hong Kong, he led a Great Compassion Dharma Assembly and then returned to Nan Hua in the fall. In 1939, the Master's one-hundredth year, there was widespread hostilities during the spring Precept Period. The new preceptees were many in number, arriving from all parts of the country. The Master recommended that everyone bow in repentance for two hours each day in order to end the disastrous plundering of the country, and also to cross over the many soldiers who had died in the war against the Japanese. He further suggested that the people in the monastery not eat after noon and turn over the food saved from their not eating dinner to the government to be used for relief. Everyone approved the Master's proposals.

The gatha says:

> He cherished compassion and benevolence
>     and aided the endangered people,
> Just like the Elder Sudatta
>     who provided for orphans and the poor.
> The grand old man of Buddhism,
>     ever thinking of the masses,
> Urged the reduction of food and clothing
>     to save his fellow beings.

助賑飢不蓄財

庚辰一百有一歲春戒後。
廣州淪陷軍民兩政各
機關還作曲江十方僧俗。
源源而來乃重修曲江
大鑑寺為南華下院又
修月華寺以廣接眼華
已一百有二歲春戒後儘
速完成各工程將所收果
資二十餘萬元文政府賑飢。
宣化偈曰
大地眾生有佛性。
德高僧善薩心大捨
布施周法界大喜寂
然入定中。

# 182

## Helping relieve the starving by not keeping any wealth for himself

The Master was one-hundred-and-one in 1940. After the spring Precept Period, Canton had already fallen, and the military and civilian governmental offices moved operations to Ch'ü Chiang. Members of the Sangha arrived in large numbers from all over, and the Master had Ta Chien (Great Brightness) Monastery of Ch'ü Chiang renovated and operated as a branch of Nan Hua Monastery. Yüeh Hua (Moon Flower) Monastery was also repaired to receive the large numbers of wandering monks. In 1941, the Master was one hundred and two years old. After the spring Precept Period, the construction was completed with utmost speed. The Master turned over more than two hundred thousand dollars from the donations he had received for reconstruction to the government in order to relieve those who were starving.

The gatha says:

> Every living being on earth
>     has the Buddha nature.
> The greatly virtuous and eminent Sanghan
>     had a Bodhisattva's heart.
> His magnanimous renunciation
>     pervaded the Dharma Realm.
> With great joy, and yet quite still,
>     he entered into samadhi.

樟樹神求受戒

壬午一百有二歲春戒期
中有一男子自稱張氏子。
世居曲江年卅四歲未出
家求戒問其剃度師是
誰曰無問其有備三衣
缽具否曰無公賜以法名
為常存緘默勤謹三壇
戒竟失踪矣次年入夢。
索戒牒公如其為樟樹。
宣化偈曰

老樟求戒六奇緣院無
牒其少師傳公問方
便賜法孫三壇受畢
竟杳然。

# 183

## Being aware that a camphor spirit
## sought the precepts

During the Spring Precept Period of 1942, the Master's one-hundred-and-third year, a man who called himself the Son of Chang, who was a native of Ch'ü Chiang and thirty-four years old, came to seek transmission of the precepts. When asked under whom he had shaved his head, he said that he did not have a Master. When asked if he had the requisite three robes and bowl, he answered that he did not. The Master then supplied him with all of the requisite items and gave him the Dharma name Ch'ang Ju (Tolerating Insult). He was quiet, diligent, and attentive. After the Three Platforms of Precepts had been transmitted, he disappeared without a trace. The following year, the Master had a vision of him asking for his Precept Certificate and immediately knew that he was in reality the spirit of a camphor tree.

The gatha says:

> The old camphor spirit sought the precepts
>     by a strange affinity,
> But since he had no bowl or robes,
>     no teacher would accept him.
> The Master opened the door of expedients
>     and gave him a Dharma name.
> All three groups of precepts once transmitted,
>     he was gone mysteriously.

# 敵機自撞焚毀

秋脩無盡庵有敵機空
中八架飛翔久之是時
政府要員多人來寺會
議國策敵偵察上空不
去公令一切人等及僧眾
歸寮勿動自至大殿拈
香趺坐敵機投彈於寺
外河边林中而自向撞
毀兩機焚燒此後敵機
不復來矣。

宣化偈曰

敵機轟炸勢猛山南華
寺上探軍情佛力護
持驅為無險全憑老僧定功

**184**

# Watching enemy aircraft collide and be demolished

In the fall, the Master renovated Wu Chin (Inexhaustible) Convent. One day, eight enemy bombers soared overhead. During this period, many senior government officials had been convening at the monastery to discuss national strategy. However, enemy intelligence had found this out, and now the bombers were hovering above the monastery and didn't go away. The Master told everyone, including the monks, to return to their rooms and not to move. He then went to the main hall, lit some incense, and sat in meditation. An enemy plane dropped a bomb which exploded outside the monastery complex on a riverbank in the grove. Then two of the bombers collided, crashed, and burned. The enemy planes never came back again.

The gatha says:

> The enemy planes' exploding bombs
>     were a violent, evil force.
> In the halls of Nan Hua Monastery
>     the military meetings had been discovered.
> Under the Buddha's aiding protection,
>     they were frightened, but not in danger,
> For all depended on the elder monk,
>     whose samadhi transformed a response.

韋陀示夢救心

冬十月林主席暨考官
員派屈映光張子廉請公
赴重慶建救國息災法會。

癸未一百有甲歲政府考官
請齋三月回南華有潮
籍鄭子嘉居士来寺云

經商於港日冠陷港夢
金甲武士指其逃難方
向今至南華見韋陀菩
薩即所夢指示方向之
神也　宣化偈曰

子夫夢韋院感恩戴
德請願修寺廟首助
海會舍。

# 185

## An account of gaining determination due to the appearance of Wei T'ou Bodhisattva

In November, Chief of State Lin, among other government officials, sent Upasakas Ch'ü Ying Kuang and Chang Tzu Lien to invite the Master to Ch'ung Ch'ing to hold a Dharma assembly for the welfare of the nation. In 1943, the Master was one-hundred-and-four, and various high government officials invited him for meals of pure food. In the third lunar month, he returned to Nan Hua Monastery. Upasaka Cheng Tzu Chia of Ch'ao Chou arrived, and explained that he was a merchant in Hong Kong. When the enemy took the city, he saw a golden armored knight, who pointed out a way for him to escape the beseiged city. Now he had come to Nan Hua Monastery, and upon seeing the statue of Wei T'ou Bodhisattva, realized that the one who had helped him escape was none other than Wei T'ou.

The gatha says:

> Wei T'ou appeared to Tzu Chia,
> Who wished to repay his gratitude.
> Making a vow to repair monasteries,
> He first helped out the Hai Hui[25] Cottage.

---

25. Sea-Assembly

黑龍怪歸正法

甲申一百有五歲江西謝雙
湖醫生送戒尼演慧來
求戒。一日過堂繞佛念審
嚴須臾醒三壇畢睨云
看黑龍怪纒身境因
得黑龍怪莫能近六請求
受戒冥戒政邪歸正豆
借身畫一黑龍像龍首人
身令演慧擎而受戒公
允之　宣化偈曰

黑龍作業亂女貞雄遂出
家仍舊侵南華受戒祈
聖者一同受戒速離
身。

# 186

## Allowing a black dragon spirit to turn to the Proper Dharma

It was 1944, the Master's one-hundred-and-fifth year, and Dr. Hsieh Shuang Hu of Chiang Hsi arrived with the newly ordained Bhikshuni Yen Hui to seek the precepts. One day, while they were circumambulating the Buddhas, a vaporous mist appeared for a moment around Yen Hui. After the transmission of the three sets of precepts, she knelt before the Master and said that a black dragon spirit had been possessing her. But now, because she had received the precepts, the dragon could not get in, and it now sought the precepts for those of the underworld. It promised to change its evil ways and to turn toward the proper. The dragon had borrowed her body and drew a picture of a black dragon with the body of a person and a dragon's head. Then the Master let Yen Hui hold up the dragon's portrait while he bestowed the precepts on the dragon's behalf.

The gatha says:

> The jet-black dragon was a spirit which
>   possessed the virgin girl.
> Although she had gone forth from home,
>   it still possessed her as before.
> At Nan Hua Temple, she received the precepts
>   and prayed to the Sage in residence.
> Both she and the dragon received the precepts,
>   and then the dragon left her body.

山蜂聚土胚来

夏南華建水陸前一月。有山蜂無數巨大及梅指結巢於法堂兩廊工精巧公偕岑學呂等視之曰人頭蜂也不常見之物。始將有事乎至十月日佔詔龍搶劫南華去後本岬時項公派人來搶岑赴雲門足見公慧物先知之妙。宣化偈曰山蜂結巢土胚束四方蜂動亂世態預言先兆語東中待至看事接汝回。

# 187

## Observing the bees swarm as the enemy arrives

During the summer, a ceremony to cross over those who had died on land or at sea was held at Nan Hua Monastery. During the previous month, a large swarm of bees, each as large as a thumb, nested in both corridors of the dining hall. They were very clever workers. The Master pointed them out to Ts'en Hsüeh Lu, and said that the bees, who had miniature human heads, were a very rare sight indeed, and that their appearance meant that danger was imminent. By the eleventh lunar month, Ch'ao Chou (Swatow) was occupied, and the enemy had attacked and desecrated Nan Hua Monastery. They left after half an hour, and the Master sent people to escort Ts'en to Yün Men Monastery. One can plainly see the wonder of the Master's accurate predictions.

The gatha says:

> The giant bees swarmed at the temple
>     and the enemy arrived.
> The movement of bees from all four directions
>     revealed the world's turmoil.
> The Master uttered a prediction.
> Expecting there would be trouble,
>     he sent Ts'en back to Yün Men.

民逃雞工免薪

乙酉一百有六歲粵北已
陷被日寇佔據逃難來寺
者甚多。初食飯粥次食
木薯粉往亂兵萬難之
際公自民卅二年由李
漢魂諸公送駐錫雲門
山大覺寺首殿俱興現
雖時局不安仍進行修
建工程而木泥瓦等匠
人六暫不領工資
宣化偈曰　離亂興工
倍艱巨更加難民增
員擔頷同甘苦與患
難丹寺工者不支錢。

# 188

## Witnessing people fleeing from trouble; workers forego wages

In 1945, the Master was one-hundred-and-six. Northern Canton Province had been invaded by and fallen to the Japanese. People fled the stricken areas, and came in large numbers to the monasteries. At first, everyone ate rice gruel, and later on just potato flour. During this very difficult period of chaos and military action, the Master had been escorted by General Li Han Yün and others to Ta Chueh (Great Enlightenment) Monastery on Yün Men (Cloud Gate) Mountain in the thirty-second year of the Republic (1944). He began to take care of the previously neglected monastery, and despite the unpeaceful times, he still went ahead with reconstruction projects. Bricklayers, stonemasons, and carpenters who were temporarily at the monastery donated their labor.

The gatha says:

> Despite the chaos, the work began
> amidst redoubled vicissitudes.
> The Master continued to aid the people;
> his heavy burden increased.
> They vowed to undergo sweetness and suffering
> and those difficult times together.
> What is more, the workers there
> did not ask for wages.

六榕緋桃瑞應

丙戌一百有七歲二次世
界大戰傳。各省復員工
作。南華仍聞戒誨經政
府通令全國各寺廟誦
經超度我爭忠魂公應
穗官紳邀請主法設壇
於淨慧寺。而時在九月
十七日內緋桃著花重
台璀璨浮未曾有。十餘
萬人
　　　宣化偈曰
有情無情皆隨喜善人
惡人盡參觀緋桃九月
放花慈。龍華三會願
相逢。

# 189

## Recording the auspicious portent of peach trees blossoming at Liu Jung[26] Monastery

The Master was one-hundred-and-seven in 1946; World War II had ended, and provincial officials returned to work. The Master transmitted the precepts at Nan Hua Monastery and explained the sutras as usual. The government requested that monasteries throughout the nation recite sutras for the welfare of the spirits of patriotic war victims. The Master responded to an invitation by Canton public officials to host the Dharma and set up an altar at Ching Hui (Pure Wisdom) Monastery. At that time, on the seventeenth day of the ninth lunar month, the peach trees inside the monastery compound prolifically blossomed with lustrous flowers. Everyone was surprised, and over a hundred thousand people came to see the rare occurrence.

The gatha says:

> Those with sentience and those without
>     joyously followed along.
> People, both good and evil,
>     came to investigate.
> The peach trees were blooming out of season
>     with clusters of buds and flowers;
> Everyone vowed to meet each other
>     in the Dragon Flower's three assemblies[27].

---

26. "Six Banyan Trees"
27. A reference to the three Dharma assemblies to be held under the Dragon Flower Tree when Maitreya, the Buddha of the future, will enter the world.

171

安慈萬里拜雲公

丁亥一百有八歲赴南華
傳戒講往後赴港澳中
山石岐等地作法會戊
子一百有九歲萬里照外
之双城安慈邇度輪者。
東親近公語次公知為法
器印証工夫見地咐囑心
印妙理命為戒學院教
務職戴器待時。
宣化偈曰
雲公見我言如是我
見雲公証及是雲公
與我皆如是晉顗眾
生點如是。

# 190

## Receiving the monk An Tz'u[28] who had traveled ten thousand *li* to pay his respects

In 1947, the Master was one-hundred-and-eight and returned to Nan Hua Monastery for the transmission of the precepts and to explain the sutras. Later, he went to Hong Kong, Macau, Chung Shan County, Shih Ch'i and many other places for Dharma assemblies. In 1948, the Master's one-hundred-and-ninth year, the monk An Tz'u (Peaceful Kindness), whose other name is To Lun (Wheel that Crosses Over), traveled more than ten thousand *li* from Shuang Ch'eng County to draw near to the Master. During their subsequent conversations, the Master recognized that the monk An Tz'u was a Dharma vessel, formally verifying his spiritual skill, charged him with the wonderful principle of the Mind-Seal. The Master told him to assume the directorship of the Vinaya Academy, storing away the vessel until the time was ripe.

The gatha says:

> The Venerable Master Yün saw me,
>     saying, "It is thus."
> I saw the Venerable Master Yün,
>     and verified, "Thus it is."
> The Venerable Master Yün and myself
>     together are both thus
> And vow that beings everywhere
>     realize they, too, are thus.

---

28. "Peaceful Kindness"

詹寧士來皈依

春戒畢。赴穗港弘法。冬
有美國居士阿難陀詹
寧士。旬美飛華。就有道
而証焉。美父母為天主教
神父。夫六教徒自研習
二十餘年。知非究竟。政習
佛義。在印掩閉四年有悟
慕公禪風而來南華皈
依法名寬弘舉行禪七
畢公興詹暨度輪禪人
攝影紀念　宣化偈曰
弟子滿大千。恒沙教不
完今舉詹寧士略以
表一端。

**191**

## Accepting Ananda Jennings to take refuge

After the annual Spring Precept Period, the Master went to Canton, and then Hong Kong, to propagate the Dharma. In the winter, an American woman named Ananda Jennings flew from the United States to China seeking to verify her understanding of the Way. This laywoman's father was a Catholic priest and she herself had studied religion as a devotee for more than twenty years. But, realizing that the goals of Catholicism were not ultimate, she changed and began to practice Buddhist principles. Later, during a four-year stay in seclusion in India, she experienced an awakening, and hearing about the Master's reputation in Ch'an practice, very much wanted to see him. So she went to Nan Hua Monastery, where she took refuge under the Master, and received the Dharma name K'uan Hung (Broad and Vast). At the conclusion of the ensuing Ch'an meditation week, the Master, Upasika Jennings, and Ch'an Master To Lun were photographed together as a memorial.

The gatha says:

> His disciples filled up thousands of worlds,
> More than the number of sands in the Ganges River.
> Here we bring up the case of Ananda Jennings,
> Who was but one of the many taught by him.

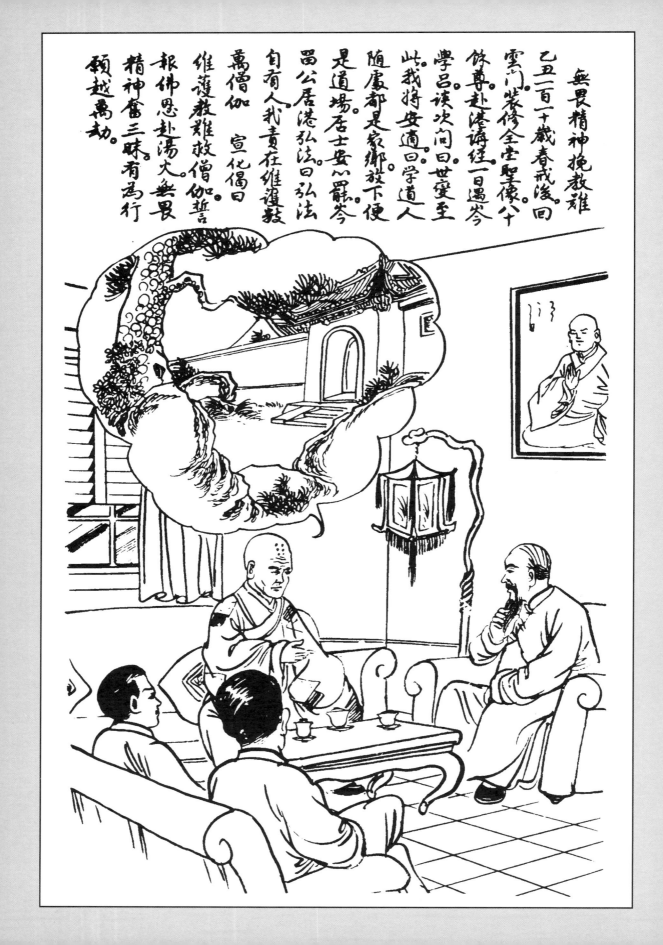

無畏精神挽救難

乙丑二百一十歲春戒後。回
雲門裝修全堂聖像八十
餘尊赴港講經一日遇岑
學呂讀次向曰世變至
此我將安適曰學道人
隨處都是家鄉教下便
是道場。曾公居士安心罷矣
岑公居士安問弘法曰弘法
自有人我責在維護教
萬僧伽　宣化偈曰
維護教難救僧伽誓
報佛恩赴湯火無畏
精神奮三昧有為行
顧越萬劫。

**192**

## Rescuing the teaching with fearless vigor

The Master was one-hundred-and-ten in 1949, and following the annual Spring Precept Period, he returned to Yün Men (Cloud Gate) Monastery, where he had crafted a full set of more than eighty sacred images. Later, he went to Hong Kong to expound Sutras, and one day met Ts'en Hsüeh Lü[29], who asked, "Where can I go to attain peace in this ever-changing world?" The Master answered, "For a student of the Way, wherever he goes is his home. Letting go of everything is just the Bodhimanda. Don't worry about it so much." Ts'en insisted the Master stay in Hong Kong to propagate the Dharma, but he said, "There are already people here who can do so. My responsibility lies in holding together the several tens of thousands of bhikshus on the Mainland."

The gatha says:

> To hold together and protect the Teaching,
>     he saved the Sangha members.
> Vowing to repay the Buddha's kindness,
>     he would go through scaldings and fire.
> With fearlessness and unfledging vigor,
>     his samadhi was energetic.
> The practice of his magnanimous vows
>     extends through thousands of kalpas.

---

[29.] See #187.

雲門驟變受奇刑

庚寅一百十一歲。仍赴南
華傳戒向雲門禪堂長
期打禪之有開悟者辛
卯一百十一歲。春戒中。雲
門驟變農曆二月曹。
突來百餘持武器者將
寺圍困驅僧眾於禪堂。
不許自由行動禁雲公
於丈室斷絕便溺飲食。
恣意搜索翻天覆地打罵
交加。　宣化偈曰
拷打索金銀眾僧不
知云。毒迫僧中瑞血
流肋斷根。

**193**

## As Yün Men suddenly changes, undergoing cruel punishment

The Master again went to Nan Hua Monastery to transmit the precepts in his one-hundred-and-eleventh year, 1950. He later returned to Yün Men Monastery and held several weeks of Ch'an meditation, during which some people gained awakenings. In 1951, the Master was one-hundred-and-twelve, and during the Spring Precept Period, Yün Men was invaded without warning. On the twenty-fourth day of the second lunar month, more than one hundred armed men suddenly appeared, surrounded the monastery, and confined the Sangha to the Dhyana Hall. No one was allowed to move. The Master Yün was detained in the Abbot's room. He was denied food and drink as well as the opportunity to relieve himself. The hoodlums ransacked the entire grounds, turning heaven and earth upside down, and subjected the residents to violent physical assault and verbal insult.

The gatha says:

> They tortured the Master,
>     looking for gold and silver.
> The Sangha did not know what to say.
> Hoodlums malevolently attacked the
>     propitious monk:
> The Master's blood flowed over
>     his broken ribs.

見慈氏歸去來

三月初三日。傷勢嚴重。仍
趺坐不視不言不食不飲。
侍者屬施雲寬純在側而圍
者屬法雲寬純在側而圍
日則吉祥臥氣絕脈停。
而體溫十二日復甦語夢
至兜率內院莊嚴瑰麗。
非世有彌勒菩薩座上
說法有志善業柏等阿
難作維那公位第三。
宣化偈曰
唯心識定法慈氏親
口宣業緣暫回去事
竟舟復還。

# 194

## Seeing "the Kindly One" and then returning

In the first three days of the third lunar month, the Master's condition was critical due to his injuries. He still sat in the meditation posture, but could no longer see, speak, eat, or drink. Two attendants, Fa Yün (Dharma Cloud) and K'uan Ch'un (Broad and Pure), were at his side, but his captors repeatedly flogged him without mercy to the point of death. By the eleventh, the Master had assumed the Auspicious Resting Posture[30]; his breath and pulse had stopped, but his body was still warm. On the twelfth, he regained consciousness and said that he had been to the inner court of the Tushita Heaven. It was adorned in the extraordinary beauty of another world. Maitreya Bodhisattva was on a throne speaking the Dharma, and Dharma Masters Chih Shan (Utmost Goodness) and Tzu Pai (Purple Cypress) were present among others. The Venerable Ananda was the wei-no, and the Master was shown to the third seat.

The gatha says:

> Mind only is the method of samadhi,
> As Maitreya himself told the Master, saying:
> "Temporarily return, due to karmic conditions.
> When affairs are over,
>     you will be able to come back here."

---

[30.] The position in which the Buddha entered Nirvana.

经调查同斩柴

至此僧众仍无自由即
食饭六受监视五月事
传至北京当局派要员
及省委等来寺调查询
目睹而已云川灾难告
问公曰无事不过耳聋
平息但食已尽公曰余
业果大众受苦无食诸
各方便去留众不去斩
柴瞒来煮粥同食功课
照常。宣化偈曰
登山斩柴薪赴市换
白米既无你我他和
合真一体。

**195**

## Going through an investigation and joining others in gathering firewood

After these events, the Sangha was denied its freedom – even their food was subject to stringent examination. In the fifth lunar month, the news of the seizure reached Peking, and the government sent public officials and county authorities to conduct an investigation at the monastery. When asked, the Master told them that nothing had happened. However, he had become deaf and blind. The seizure of Yün Men Monastery gradually relaxed, but the food supply was entirely gone. The Master commented, "Because my karma has involved all of you, now you must suffer going without food. You are now free to come or go." But the community refused to go. They sold firewood to buy rice, which everyone ate together. The work went on as usual.


The gatha says:

> Climbing the hills to gather firewood,
> They went to the market and exchanged it for rice.
> Since there is no you, me, or others,
> True harmony of single substance prevailed.

出雲門進北京

壬辰一百十三歲春公傷
病稍瘥領銀安禪行道。
雙殘局正月至三月北
京四次電請公北行專
員護送公告報回時機
至矣為挽救難義當如
此乃書聯云坐閱五帝
四朝不覺滄桑戊慶受
盡九磨十難了知世事
無常四月初四日能四侍
者北上　宣化偈曰
公願赴北平挽教救
尼僧十方大團結一
致力實行

**196**

## Going to Peking from Yün Men

The Master's injuries improved slightly in 1952, his one-hundred-and-thirteenth year, as he led the assembly sitting in dhyana meditation, practicing the Way, and readjusting to the aftermath. The government in Peking telegraphed four times between the first and third lunar months, requesting the Master to come to Peking. Officers were sent to accompany him, and he told the community: "The time has come for me to go, for the Teachings are in difficulty..." He composed a matched couplet, which reads:

> Five emperors and four dynasties
>     have passed me by,
> And yet the changes gone with them,
>     I know not how to measure.
> Completely worn through
>     by the nine tribulations and ten difficulties,
> I thoroughly know the impermanence
>     of worldly affairs.

On the fourth day of the fourth lunar month, he headed north with four attendants.

The gatha says:

> The Master vowed to go to Peking
> To rescue the Teachings and the Sangha,
> To join the groups of the ten directions,
> Through the strength of united cultivation.

三佛寺觀音七

抵韶州時。千餘善信迎
於十里之外。住大鑑寺。
參禪者塞途。初十日附
粵漢車北上至武昌。住
三佛寺。是瘡慶陳真如
為理醫藥稍瘥應慈知
尚請建觀音七皈依二
千餘人法事竟將扶病
北行時衆請攝影留為
紀念　宣化偈曰
老病驅馳為衆忙
志浩慇凌霜壯途程
三佛當道影丹心一
點報法王。

## 197

## Leading a Kuan Yin session
## at San Fo Monastery

When they arrived at Ch'ao Chou, more than a thousand faithful people welcomed the Master ten *li* outside the city. He stayed at Ta Chien (Great Brightness) Monastery, and people who wished to bow to him clogged the roads. On the tenth, they took the Canton Hankow train north, and stayed at San Fo (Three Buddhas) Monastery when they arrived at Wu Ch'ang. Ch'en Chen Ju arranged for a doctor to treat the Master's painful wounds, and his condition improved slightly. He agreed to Abbot Hsin's request that he hold a Kuan Yin session, during which more than two thousand people took refuge. When the ceremonies ended, he continued north, despite his illness. The assembly requested that a group photograph be taken as a memorial.

The gatha says:

> Old and infirmed, he still made the trip
> to help the great assembly.
> His great resolve was strong indeed,
> connecting heaven and earth.
> Passing through Three Buddhas Monastery,
> their picture was taken.
> With a heart of utmost loyalty,
> he sought to repay the Dharma King.

抵京駐錫廣濟寺

公題詩云業風吹送到
武昌老病馳驅累眾忙。
三月淹留三佛寺一場
災難一慚惶無心歌跨
樓頭想玉泉鵠有願同登選佛
場尚想玉泉崗壯總餘
於言下悟真常七月廿
八日附京漢車北進抵
京諸山長老各團體李
任潮葉退庵等迎接先往
廣化後移錫廣濟寺
宣化偈曰　末法人心危。
聖僧道心微千古重功
勳萬世仰光輝。

# 198

## Arriving at the capital and staying at Kuang Chi[31] Monastery

The Master wrote a verse which says:

> The karmic wind arises now and
>     blows me to Wu Ch'ang,
> Where my advancing illness and age
>     inveigles everyone else.
> Tarrying long for three full months
>     at Three Buddhas Monastery,
> I feel embarrassed at all this misery.
> I have no desire to surpass the crane[32]
>     on a high rooftop;
> My vow is that we together ascend
>     the Way Place where Buddhas are selected,
> As I ever think of Jade Spring Mountain
>     and General Kuan Chuang Niu[33],
> Who awakened to the genuine truth
>     at the fall of a single word.

On the twenty-eighth day of the seven lunar month, they took the Peking-Hankow train north to the capital. All of the elders from the monasteries, various Buddhist groups, and others, such as Upasaka Li Jen Ch'ao and Yeh T'ui An, were there to welcome the Master. At first he stayed at Kuang Hua (Vast Influence) Monastery, and then moved to Kuang Chi (Extensive Aid) Monastery. The gatha says:

> The mind of man is in danger during this
>     Dharma-ending age,
> But the heart of the Sagely Sanghan's Way was subtle.
> He was steeped in a thousand years of merit,
> And ten thousand generations will
>     look up to his resplendent light.

---

[31.] "Extensive Aid"
[32.] A symbol of longevity
[33.] A well-known general of the Three Kingdoms Period in China (A.D. 222-265), who received the Precepts from Great Master Chih Che (Wise One)

代全国接受三宝

由圆瑛等在广济寺成
立中国佛教协会筹备
处，拟举公为会长公以
老病辞乃住名誉会长。
上书当局（一）无论何地。
不许再拆寺院。毁佛焚
经（二）不许强迫僧尼还
俗（三）寺产收归公有后。
仍应按僧配给田亩若干
自种生产许之代表接受
锡兰赠三宝。

宣化偈曰　佛陀舍利子。
贝叶达磨继菩提道宝。
树我师亲手迎。

## 199

## Accepting three gifts on behalf of the nation

Along with Dharma Master Yüan Ying and others, the Master formed the Chinese Buddhist Association at Kuang Chi (Extensive Aid) Monastery. The Master was nominated for the office of President, but he declined because of old age and ill health and assumed the title of Honorary President. The following resolutions were proposed to the government: 1) In all places, further destruction of monasteries and temples, the desecration of images, and the burning of sutras shall immediately cease; 2) the intimidation of bhikshus and bhikshunis to force their return to lay life will not be tolerated; and 3) all monastery property shall be returned forthwith, and there should be returned to the Sangha enough arable acreage to make the monasteries self-supporting. The petition was approved. The Master then represented the Association in receiving three gifts from a Buddhist delegation from Sri Lanka.

The gatha says:

> The Buddha's sharira,
> A sutra written on a palm leaf,
> The jeweled tree of the path of Bodhi:
> Our teacher personally received.

世界和平大法會

十月滬眾起祝願世界和平法會。眾議請公主法派方子藩等迎請十二月十一日抵滬扴旗獻花者千餘眾法會定農曆十月廿六日啟建水陸並請應慈靜權等十大德副之僧眾七十二人至十二月十四日圓滿參謁者如潮宣化偈曰
法會祈求世和平道
場珠勝各安寧消災
免劫彌戾氣增福延
壽降吉星。

# 200

## Hosting a Great Dharma Assembly
## for world peace

In the tenth lunar month, the people of Shanghai decided to convene a Dharma assembly for world peace. They met and requested the Master to be the Dharma Host. Fang Tzu Fan and others were sent to invite and escort him. They returned to Shanghai on the eleventh, and more than a thousand people waving flags and offering flowers welcomed the Master. The meeting was set for the twenty-sixth day of the tenth lunar month, and ceremonies for the welfare of creatures both on land and in the water were held. Dharma Masters Ying Tz'u and Ching Ch'üan, among ten eminent monks, were requested to assist, and seventy-two other monks took part. The assembly lasted until the fourteenth of the twelfth lunar month and participants swarmed the Way-place.

The gatha says:

> The purpose of the Dharma Assembly
> was to pray for peace in the world.
> The Bodhimanda was most supreme,
> and all in it were at ease.
> Ending disaster and stopping war,
> they did away with violence.
> Blessings increased and lives were lengthened
> – an auspicious star had descended.

皈依供眾名剎僧。

法會皈依者四萬餘人。有全國各省暨千里之外者。分設十席報名登記。分班給牒所投求敬。

盡玄法會當局自己分文不受。概撰典四大名山供眾計有普陀山五台山九華山峨嵋山八名剎天童育王高旻靈巖湧泉觀宗七塔地藏等古道場。宣化偈曰博施能濟眾孔曰惟聖當供養古名剎功德永流芳。

# 201

## Accepting a collective offering made by those taking refuge for the Sangha and for the preservation of ancient shrines

More than forty thousand people took refuge during the Dharma Assembly, coming thousands of miles from every province all over the country. Ten divisions were formed so that people could register and subscriptions be entered. The Master refused to accept any offerings himself, and all the donations were turned over to the leaders of the Dharma Assembly, who in turn allocated the funds to the four famous shrines for the benefit of all, namely: P'u T'ou Mountain, Wu T'ai Mountain, Chiu Hua (Nine Flower) Mountain, and O-Mei Mountain, in addition to eight well-known holy sites: T'ien T'ung (Heavenly Youth), Yü Wang (King Ashoka), Kao Min, Ling Yen (Magic Grotto), Yung Ch'üan (Bubbling Spring), Kuan Tsung (School of Contemplation), Ch'i T'a (Seven Stupas), and Ti Tsang (Earth Store), among other ancient Bodhimandas.

The gatha says:

> Liberal gifts can help relieve the masses.
> Confucius said that only a Sage
> could make that happen.
> Making offerings to ancient holy shrines,
> Creates merit that flows ever-fresh.

蘇杭法會重重

癸巳一百一西歲在玉佛
寺。正月初九日起禪七西
個。旋杭州佛教團體派
杜偉來請。赴杭主持法
會住淨慈寺。皈依者數
千。又應妙真之請赴蘇
州舉行法會畢遊虎邱。
禮紹隆祖塔見已毀殘
起令人重建之以重名
勝　宣化偈曰
杭州事畢至姑蘇法會
重重不休。虎邱母禮
紹祖塔。毀而復只緒
千秋。

**202**

## Hosting Dharma Assemblies at Su Chou and Hang Chou one after another

In 1953, at one-hundred-and-fourteen years of age, the Master began a two-week meditation session on the ninth day of the first lunar month at Yü Fo (Jade Buddha) Monastery. Upon its conclusion, the Hang Chou Buddhist Group sent Tu Wei to invite the Master to go to Hang Chou and take charge of a Dharma assembly. He accepted and stayed at Ching Tzu (Pure Kindness) Monastery, where several thousand people took refuge. Again, the Master responded to a request by Dharma Master Miao Chen (Wonderful Truth) that he hold a Dharma assembly. When it was over, the Master proceeded to Hu Ch'iu (Tiger Mountain), and bowed to the stupa of Patriarch Shao Lung. Seeing that it had been desecrated, he saw to its reconstruction, and it again became a famous site.

The gatha says:

> When affairs in Hang Chou were completed
>     the Master went to Ku Su,
> Conducting Dharma assemblies one after another,
>     never stopping to rest.
> At Hu Ch'iu he once again bowed to the Stupa of
>     Patriach Shao Lung (Propagate and Glorify).
> It had been destroyed, but he now rebuilt it
>     to last for a thousand seasons.

参云岗石佛

公应南通请於狼山主
持法会各地皈依均数
千人。三月晦回沪四月
接北京电请进京仍居
广济寺各地佛教代表六至
中国佛教协会正式成立。
大会议决各要案後公
赴山西大同参礼云岗
大石佛崛诚美化伟大。
艺术雕刻　宣化偈回
艺术精雕云岗佛举
世皆称伟大作。我师
最後元朝礼率身
垂範勿空过。

# 203

## Visiting the Stone Buddhas at Yün Kang

The Master responded to the invitation of Dharma Master Nan T'ung (Penetration to the South) to head another Dharma assembly at Lang Shan (Wolf Mountain) Monastery, where several thousand people from all over took refuge. He returned to Shanghai in the third lunar month, and the next month received a telegram from Peking requesting his presence in the capital. The Master arrived and stayed at Kuang Chi (Extensive Aid) Monastery. Representatives of various Buddhist groups also were present, and the Chinese Buddhist Association was officially inaugurated. After a plenary meeting in which important policies were decided, the Master went to Ta T'ung in Shanhsi Province and bowed to the large stone Buddhas in the stone grottos at Yün Kang. They were quite imposing and magnificently carved.

The gatha says:

> The Buddhas at the Yün Kang (Cloud Ridge) Caves
>     are skillfully and finely made.
> They are known throughout the world
>     and acclaimed for their inspiring grandeur.
> Our Master Yün especially made
>     a pilgrimage to bow there.
> Conducting himself as an exemplar of the rule,
>     he never wasted a moment.

念祖功重建古刹

旋離京赴武昌。源成師
請於寶通主禪七之期
畢至盧山住東林寺。六
月有教禪人自永修靈
居來拜言日寇時將真
如寺焚毀僅存毗盧遮
那佛銅像魏魏坐於荒
煙漫草中。公凄然念旬
唐元和道容祖師開山
倍出宗匠常重興之。
宣化偈曰　雲居真如
雲公居慈悲三昧慈
母慈祖師道場譬重
建菩薩行願無已時。

# 204

## Mindful of the Patriarchs' merit, reestablishing an ancient shrine

After leaving the capital, the Master traveled to Wu Ch'ang, where Dharma Master Yüan Ch'eng (Source Formation) invited him to head a two-week Ch'an meditation session in Pao T'ung (Jeweled Penetration) Monastery. When it was over, the Master visited Lü Shan Mountain, staying in Tung Lin (Eastern Grove) Monastery. In the sixth lunar month, several Dhyana monks from Yün (Cloud Abode) Mountain in Yung Hsiu came to bow in reverence to the Master. They told him that, during the invasion, the Japanese had burned and destroyed Chen Ju (True Suchness) Monastery, leaving only a bronze image of Vairochana Buddha majestically sitting amidst the waste of ashes and overgrown grass. The Master sadly recalled how, during the Yüan Ho Reign of the T'ang Dynasty (806 A.D.), the Patriarch Tao Jung (Acceptance of the Way) had established the monastic community there. So the Master craftsman of Buddhism undertook yet another renovation.

The gatha says:

> The Master Yün dwelt
> on Yün Chu[34]Mountain at Chen Ju[35]
> The compassion of his lucid samadhi was
> like a mother's deep concern,
> As he once again vowed to restore
> the Patriarch's Bodhimanda.
> The practice and vows of a Bodhisattva never end!

---

[34.] Cloud Abode
[35.] True Suchness Monastery

雲居結茆而居

七月初五日入雲居山居
於牛欄九月間有粵徒
眾至十方海眾已五十餘
人十月各處僧伽禪和源
源間風而至益多食宿
兩緊幸得間玉階施助。
甲午一百十五歲公即籌建
僧坊教樹法堂一幢大殿
等十一月牛欄焚結茆而
居起禪七。

宣化偈曰　結茆安居
心地廣古石趺坐性天
寬雲公至此全教下。
不休々時六休休。

**205**

## Staying in a shack on Yün Chü Mountain

On the fifth day of the seventh lunar month, the Master arrived at Yün Chü (Cloud Abode) Mountain, and stayed in a cow shed. During the ninth lunar month, several left-home disciples from Canton arrived among the more than fifty monks from all over the country. By the tenth lunar month, word had spread far and wide, and monks arrived in large numbers. They ate twice a day and were fortunate enough to receive a donation from Upasaka Chien Yü Chieh. In 1954, the Master was one-hundred-and-fifteen and was in the process of repairing several dwelling quarters, the Dharma Hall, and the Main Hall of the monastery complex. In the eleventh lunar month, his cow shed burned down, but he had it rebuilt and remained living there. A meditation session was then held.

The gatha says:

> Living peacefully in a shack,
>     the ground of his mind was vast.
> Sitting full lotus on an ancient rock,
>     his faculties expanded.
> The Master Yün had reached the point
>     where he had put down everything;
> Even though he never rested, still,
>     he took a rest.

示現病相臥吉祥

乙未一百十六歲建香積
厨五觀堂等工程起禪
七一期丙申一百十七歲函
編者令赴雲居來往建
大殿天王殿等工程海
燈接住持請經起禪七
二期丁酉一百十八歲各
堂工竣造佛像百餘尊。
講經起禪七三期住僧二
百餘戊戌一百十九歲參勵
吾助建海會塔己亥一百
二十歲夏秋病劇。
宣化曰
化竟放下歸去來。

# 206

## Becoming ill and assuming the auspicious resting posture

In 1955, the Master, at one-hundred-and-sixteen, had completed the Accumulation of Fragrance Kitchen, the Five Contemplations Hall, and other construction projects, and held another meditation session. In the next year, the Master's one-hundred-and-seventeenth, he wrote a letter to the composer of this book, asking the latter to return to Yün Chü which, however, was impossible. The Great Hall and the Hall of the Heavenly Kings were completed, in addition to other monastery buildings, and Dharma Master Hai Teng (Sea Lamp) became Abbot. The Master continued to lecture Sutras and held a two-week meditation session. In 1957, when the Master was one hundred and eighteen, all of the work was completed, and more than one hundred Buddha images were cast. The Master continued to lecture the Sutras and held a three-week meditation session. There were now more than two hundred monks living at the monastery. At one-hundred and nineteen, in 1958, the Master was aided in the establishment of the Hai Hui (Sea-vast Assembly) Stupa by Chan Li Wu. In 1959, the Master's age was one-hundred-and-twenty, and he became ill during the summer and fall.

It is said:

> "His teaching ended,
>     he put it all down and returned."

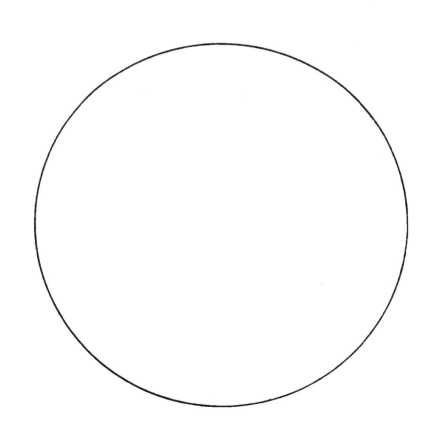

大般涅槃証無生

農曆九月十二日預知時至偽人努力精進勤修。

戒定慧息滅貪瞋痴為法忘軀互相敦勉而說偈曰。

蝛蛆蟻命不投水吾慰水族身擲江祈諸受我身願。

供同爾蘭會選不休因閒憂喜歡除此患眾生死循素如

委傅菩提度眾生請各法侶不必憂慮生死循素如

契無生明通心地斷塵憎情脫輪迴陰食淨三學堅持

四念裝願圓成質幻露電証悟真空高法一乘飛合

悲歡隨緣泡水吾死後化身畢請各侶持吾骨灰礦

成細末以油糖麵共骨灰和好做成丸棄請送放河

中以供水族滿吾所願感謝無盡還債人盧雲

頂禮。　入涅槃於己亥年甲戌月戊辰日未時

也　宣化偈曰　百廿歸去般涅槃千萬

再來度忍堪一切有情皆翹首此

民無願不重贍祈公滿眾願。

**207**

## His Parinirvana:
## certification to non production

On the twelfth day of the ninth lunar month, he knew that the time had
come. The Master instructed his successors to earnestly and vigorously
apply themselves to the cultivation of precepts, samadhi, and wisdom,
in order to counteract greed, anger, and stupidity. Telling them to forget
themselves for the sake of the Dharma and to mutually cherish and
respect one another, he then spoke the following gathas:

> A shrimp on land, covered with ants,
>> does not jump back into the water.
> As I wish to make water creatures happy,
>> toss me into the river.
> I would be pleased if they would receive
>> my body as an offering,
> So that together they'll be certified to
>> Bodhi and save living beings.

* * *

> Companions and friends in the Dharma, please
>> Do not worry, set your minds at ease.
> Life and death arise from karma
>> Just as the silkworm is trapped in its own cocoon.
> If you do not lessen greed and confusion,
>> Then you are imprisoned by worry and joy,
> If you want to get out of this tribulation,
>> Work very hard at your own cultivation.
> Wonderfully mesh with non-production;
>> With bright understanding,
>>> penetrate to the mind-ground.

> Cutting off feelings of love and of hate,
>> Escape from the wheel before it's too late.
> The triple non-outflow study must be attained,[36]
>> And the Four Applications of Mindfulness

遠個和漢有善來由
末法無端為何出頭
嗟嗟聖眷一覽危杭
拋卻已筆身為人憂
何敢峯頂直釣釣鯉
入大海底撥火煎沼
不復如青徒自縈戀
笑破虛空寫不抑留
處個猿為何不放下
蒼生苦畫即時末

何詩記以
虛宗何廬

strictly maintained.[37]
Vow to protect the precepts, too,
    Even though all is illusory lightning and dew.
Be certified as enlightened to true emptiness,
    And the ten thousand dharmas' oneness.
The sorrow and joy of coming and going,
    are just causes flowing,
        like bubbles shifting on water.

After my death, have my body cremated. Take the ashes of my bones and grind them into a fine powder. Add oil, sugar, flour, and mix. Please form them into pellets and deposit them in the rivers as an offering for the creatures therein. This will fulfill my vow, and towards all of you I will feel unlimited gratitude.

Hsü Yün, one who repays his debts,
bows in reverence.

* * *

The Master entered Nirvana on the day Wu Ch'en of the month of Chia Hsü, in the year Chi Hai[38], between 1:00 and 3:00 p.m.

The gatha says:

After one hundred and twenty years,
    he entered Parinirvana.
For thousands of years into the future,
    Please, under all circumstances, come
        again to save those in the Saha.
All sentient beings together
    raise up their heads in admiration;
None of the masses could have enough
    of gazing up at him.
May the Master fulfill
    the multitude's wishes!

---

[36.] precepts, samadhi, and wisdom
[37.] Four Applications of Mindfulness: a) to contemplate the body as impure; b) to contemplate feelings as suffering; c) to contemplate thoughts as impermanent; d) to contemplate dharmas as being devoid of self.
[38.] October 13, 1959

建大般若法會迴

度輪九月十五日閒訊十六日
召集全體護法開會議
決十七日起念佛七三期。
眾參加者甚眾十月初十
日起七誦大般若經六百
卷。為期一百四十日越年
三月初一日圓滿壇設毘盧
地成和道一誦念國大
廈土橋佛教講堂四眾隨
喜踴躍又派人迎請舍利。
建塔供養。　宣化偈曰
痛我天人師上師成彼淨土
聖中聖惟望懺悔生有生
再東來度化眾生壬申六月

# 208

## A Great Prajna Dharma Assembly is established for dedication of merit

On the fifteenth day of the ninth lunar month, Dharma Master To Lun received the news of the Master's Parinirvana and called a meeting of all protectors of the Dharma on the sixteenth. It was decided that starting on the seventeenth, a three-week Buddha recitation session would be held. The session was very well attended by bhikshus, bhikshunis, upasakas, and upasikas. On the tenth day of the tenth lunar month, a session in which the *Six Hundred Chapter Great Prajna Paramita Sutra* was continuously recited for one hundred and forty days. It was completed on the first day of the third lunar month of the following year. A memorial altar was set up at the Buddhist Lecture Hall, 31 Wong Nei Chung Road, 11<sup>th</sup> Floor, Suite A, of the Yü Yüan Building in Hong Kong. Many people joyously took part, and a person was sent to bring back the Master's sharira to enshrine in a stupa for veneration.

The gatha says:

> To the sorrow of all people and gods,
>     our master-surpassing Master
> Is now dwelling in the Pure Land,
>     a Sage among the Sages.
> May he take pity on all living beings,
> And come again to teach and save both
>     sentient and insentient beings!

# White Universe

The Venerable Master composed the poem "White Universe" on February 15, 1972, during a session for recitation of the Six-syllable Great Bright Mantra (Om mani padme hum) at Gold Mountain Dhyana Monastery. The fourfold assembly of disciples sincerely recited around the clock without fatigue, praying for world peace. Upon completion of the seven-day session, the Venerable Master was inspired to compose this poem. "White Universe" signifies that the entire universe has been purified, so that it is luminous and immaculately white. In order for the universe to be free from defilement, we must cultivate vigorously and begin by "sparing neither blood nor sweat, and never pausing to rest."

Ice in the sky, snow on the ground.
Numberless tiny bugs die in the cold
   or sleep in hibernation.
In the midst of stillness you should contemplate,
   and within movement you should investigate.
Dragons spar and tigers
   wrestle in continual playful sport;
Ghosts cry and spirits wail,
   their illusory transformations strange.
Ultimate truth transcends words;
Not thought about or talked about,
   you ought to advance with haste.
With great and small destroyed, with no inside or out,
It pervades every mote of dust
   and encompasses the Dharma Realm,
Complete, whole, and perfectly fused,

interpenetrating without obstruction.
With two clenched fists,
   shatter the covering of empty space.
In one mouthful,
   swallow the source of seas of Buddhalands.
With great compassion rescue all,
Sparing neither blood nor sweat,
   and never pause to rest!

# Buddhist Text Translation Society Publication

---

## Buddhist Text Translation Society
## International Translation Institute

http://www.bttsonline.org

1777 Murchison Drive,
Burlingame, California 94010-4504 USA
Phone: 650-692-5912 Fax: 650-692-5056

When Buddhism first came to China from India, one of the most important tasks required for its establishment was the translation of the Buddhist scriptures from Sanskrit into Chinese. This work involved a great many people, such as the renowned monk National Master Kumarajiva (fifth century), who led an assembly of over 800 people to work on the translation of the Tripitaka (Buddhist canon) for over a decade. Because of the work of individuals such as these, nearly the entire Buddhist Tripitaka of over a thousand texts exists to the present day in Chinese.

Now the banner of the Buddha's Teachings is being firmly planted in Western soil, and the same translation work is being done from Chinese into English. Since 1970, the Buddhist Text Translation Society (BTTS) has been making a paramount contribution toward this goal. Aware that the Buddhist Tripitaka is a work of such magnitude that its translation could never be entrusted to a single person, the BTTS, emulating the translation assemblies of ancient times, does not publish a work until it has passed through four committees for primary translation, revision, editing, and certification. The leaders of these committees are Bhikshus (monks) and Bhikshunis (nuns) who have devoted their lives to the study and practice of the Buddha's teachings. For this reason, all of the works of the BTTS put an emphasis on what the principles of the Buddha's teachings mean in terms of actual practice and not simply hypothetical conjecture.

The translations of canonical works by the Buddhist Text Translation Society are accompanied by extensive commentaries by the Venerable Tripitaka Master Hsuan Hua.

## BTTS Publications

**Buddhist Sutras.** Amitabha Sutra, Dharma Flower (Lotus) Sutra, Flower Adornment (Avatamsaka) Sutra, Heart Sutra & Verses without a Stand, Shurangama Sutra, Sixth Patriarch Sutra, Sutra in Forty-two Sections, Sutra of the Past Vows of Earth Store Bodhisattva, Vajra Prajna Paramita (Diamond) Sutra.

**Commentarial Literature.** Buddha Root Farm, City of 10 000 Buddhas Recitation Handbook, Filiality: The Human Source, Herein Lies the Treasure-trove, Listen to Yourself Think Everything Over, Shastra on the Door to Understanding the Hundred Dharmas, Song of Enlightenment, The Ten Dharma Realms Are Not Beyond a Single Thought, Venerable Master Hua's Talks on Dharma, Venerable Master Hua's Talks on Dharma during the 1993 Trip to Taiwan, Water Mirror Reflecting Heaven.

**Biographical.** In Memory of the Venerable Master Hsuan Hua, Pictorial Biography of the Venerable Master Hsü Yün, Records of High Sanghans, Records of the Life of the Venerable Master Hsüan Hua, Three Steps One Bow, World Peace Gathering, News from True Cultivators, Open Your Eyes Take a Look at the World, With One Heart Bowing to the City of 10 000 Buddhas.

**Children's Books.** Cherishing Life, Human Roots: Buddhist Stories for Young Readers, Spider Web, Giant Turtle, Patriarch Bodhidharma.

**Musics, Novels and Brochures.** Songs for Awakening, Awakening, The Three Cart Patriarch, City of 10 000 Buddhas Color Brochure, Celebrisi's Journey, Lots of Time Left.

**The Buddhist Monthly–Vajra Bodhi Sea** is a monthly journal of orthodox Buddhism which has been published by the Dharma Realm Buddhist Association, formerly known as the Sino-American Buddhist Association, since 1970. Each issue contains the most recent translations of the Buddhist canon by the Buddhist Text Translation Society. Also included in each issue are a biography of a great Patriarch of Buddhism from the ancient past, sketches of the lives of contemporary monastics and lay-followers around the world, articles on practice, and other material. The journal is bilingual, Chinese and English

Please visit our web-site at **www.bttsonline.org** for the latest publications and for ordering information.

# Dharma Realm Buddhist Association Branches

**The City of Ten Thousand Buddhas**
P.O. Box 217,  Talmage, CA 95481-0217 USA
Tel: (707) 462-0939   Fax: (707) 462-0949
Home Page: **http://www.drba.org**

**Institute for World Religions (Berkeley Buddhist Monastery)**
2304 McKinley Avenue, Berkeley, CA 94703 USA
Tel: (510) 848-3440

**Dharma Realm Buddhist Books Distribution Society**
11th Floor, 85 Chung-hsiao E. Road, Sec. 6, Taipei, Taiwan R.O.C.
Tel: (02) 2786-3022  Fax: (02) 2786-2674

**The City of the Dharma Realm**
1029 West Capitol Avenue, West Sacramento, CA 95691 USA
Tel: (916) 374-8268

**Gold Mountain Monastery**
800 Sacramento Street, San Francisco, CA 94108 USA
Tel: (415) 421-6117  Fax: (415) 788-6001

**Gold Wheel Monastery**
235 North Avenue 58, Los Angeles, CA 90042 USA
Tel: (323) 258-6668

**Gold Buddha Monastery**
248 East 11th Avenue, Vancouver, B.C. V5T 2C3 Canada
Tel: (604) 709-0248  Fax: (604) 684-3754

**Gold Summit Monastery**
233 1st Avenue, West Seattle, WA 98119 USA
Tel: (206) 284-6690  Fax: (206) 284-6918

**Gold Sage Monastery**
11455 Clayton Road, San Jose, CA 95127 USA
Tel: (408) 923-7243  Fax: (408) 923-1064

**The International Translation Institute**
1777 Murchison Drive, Burlingame, CA 94010-4504 USA
Tel: (650) 692-5912  Fax: (650) 692-5056

**Long Beach Monastery**
3361 East Ocean Boulevard, Long Beach, CA 90803 USA
Tel: (562) 438-8902

**Blessings, Prosperity, & Longevity Monastery**
4140 Long Beach Boulevard, Long Beach, CA 90807 USA
Tel: (562) 595-4966

**Avatamsaka Hermitage**
11721 Beall Mountain Road, Potomac, MD 20854-1128 USA
Tel: (301) 299-3693

**Avatamsaka Monastery**
1009 4th Avenue, S.W. Calgary, AB T2P OK8 Canada
Tel: (403) 234-0644

**Kun Yam Thong Temple**
161, Jalan Ampang, 50450 Kuala Lumpur, Malaysia
Tel: (03) 2164-8055  Fax: (03) 2163-7118

**Prajna Guanyin Sagely Monastery (formerly Tze Yun Tung)**
Batu 5½, Jalan Sungai Besi,
Salak Selatan, 57100 Kuala Lumpur, Malaysia
Tel: (03) 7982-6560  Fax: (03) 7980-1272

**Lotus Vihara**
136, Jalan Sekolah, 45600 Batang Berjuntai,
Selangor Darul Ehsan, Malaysia
Tel: (03) 3271-9439

**Buddhist Lecture Hall**
31 Wong Nei Chong Road, Top Floor, Happy Valley, Hong Kong, China
Tel: (02) 2572-7644

**Dharma Realm Sagely Monastery**
20, Tong-hsi Shan-chuang, Hsing-lung Village, Liu-kuei
Kaohsiung County, Taiwan, R.O.C.
Tel: (07) 689-3717  Fax: (07) 689-3870

**Amitabha Monastery**
7, Su-chien-hui, Chih-nan Village, Shou-feng,
Hualien County, Taiwan, R.O.C.
Tel: (07) 865-1956  Fax: (07) 865-3426

# Verse of Transference

May the merit and virtue accrued from this work,
Adorn the Buddhas' Pure Lands,
Repaying four kinds of kindness above,
And aiding those suffering in the paths below.

May those who see and hear of this,
All bring forth the resolve for Bodhi,
And when this retribution body is over,
Be born together in the Land of Ultimate Bliss.

Dharma Protector Wei Tuo Bodhisattva